EXCEL FOR DUMMIES™

Quick Reference

by John Walkenbach
Preface by Series Editor Dan Gookin

IDG BOOKS

IDG Books Worldwide, Inc.
An International Data Group Company

San Mateo, California ♦ Indianapolis, Indiana ♦ Boston, Massachusetts

Excel For Dummies Quick Reference

Published by
IDG Books Worldwide, Inc.
An International Data Group Company
155 Bovet Road, Suite 310
San Mateo, CA 94402

Library of Congress Catalog Card No.: 93-78449

ISBN 1-56884-028-4

Printed in the United States of America

10 9 8 7 6 5 4 3 2 1

Distributed in the United States by IDG Books Worldwide, Inc.

Distributed in Canada by Macmillan of Canada, a Division of
Canada Publishing Corporation; by Woodslane Pty. Ltd. in Austra-
lia and New Zealand; and by Computer Bookshops in the U.K. and
Ireland.

For information on translations and availability in other countries,
contact Marc Jeffrey Mikulich, Foreign Rights Manager, at IDG
Books Worldwide; FAX NUMBER 415-358-1260.

For sales inquiries and special prices for bulk quantities, write to
the address above or call IDG Books Worldwide at 415-312-0650.

 is a trademark of IDG Books Worldwide, Inc.

COMPUTER
BOOK SERIES
FROM IDG

Acknowledgments

Thanks to all the good people at IDG Books who helped transform hundreds of thousands of bytes on my hard disk into a real book: Janna Custer for choosing me to write it, Diane Steele and Sara Black for editing it, and all the others behind the scenes who pulled it all together. Thanks also to *InfoWorld*'s Bob Garza for another superb technical review and to the Production staff making it look good. Finally, I wish to acknowledge my friends Lori (a loyal Excel user) and Kelsey (a loyal Rodney's Funscreen user) who provided good times and laughs in between my keystrokes.

John Walkenbach
La Jolla, California

(The publisher would like to give special thanks to Patrick J. McGovern, without whom this book would not have been possible.)

Credits

Publisher
David Solomon

Acquisitions Editor
Janna Custer

Managing Editor
Mary Bednarek

Project Editor
Diane Graves Steele

Editor
Sara Black

Technical Reviewer
Victor R. Garza

Production Manager
Beth J. Baker

Production Coordinator
Cindy L. Phipps

Proofreader
Charles A. Hutchinson

Production Staff
Joseph A. Augsburger
Mary Breidenbach
Drew R. Moore

Indexer
Sherry Massey

A Call to Readers:

We want to hear from you!

Listen up, all you readers of IDG's *Excel For Dummies Quick Reference.*It is time for you to take advantage of a new, direct pipeline for readers of IDG's international bestsellers — the famous . . . *For Dummies* books.

We would like your input for future printings and editions of this book. Tell us what you liked (and didn't like) about the *Excel For Dummies Quick Reference*.

We'll add you to our *Dummies Database/Fan Club* and keep you up to date on the latest . . . *For Dummies* books, news, cartoons, calendars, and more!

Please send your name, address, and phone number, as well as your comments, questions, and suggestions, to:

. . . For Dummies Coordinator
IDG Books Worldwide
3250 North Post Road, Suite 140
Indianapolis, Indiana 46226

Thanks for your input!

About the Author

John Walkenbach has used spreadsheets for more than a decade, beginning with the old dinosaur of a program known as VisiCalc. He's a contributing editor for *PC World* and *InfoWorld,* co-author of the *PC World 1-2-3 for Windows Complete Handbook* and the *PC World Excel 4 for Windows Handbook,* and author of *Quattro Pro For Dummies* and *1-2-3 For Dummies Quick Reference,* all from IDG Books. He holds a Ph.D. in experimental psychology from the University of Montana and has worked as an instructor, programmer, consultant, and market research manager in the banking industry. When he's not writing about computers and software, he's probably playing around in his MIDI studio, working on his latest music-oriented shareware creation, or annoying his neighbors with weird synthetic sounds.

About the Series Editor

Dan Gookin, the author of *DOS For Dummies, DOS For Dummies, 2nd Edition, WordPerfect For Dummies, WordPerfect 6 For Dummies,* and co-author of *PCs For Dummies* and the *Illustrated Computer Dictionary For Dummies,* is a writer and computer "guru" whose job is to remind everyone that computers are not to be taken too seriously. Presently, Mr. Gookin works for himself as a freelance writer. Gookin holds a degree in Communications from the University of California, San Diego, and is a regular contributor to *InfoWorld, PC/Computing, DOS Resource Guide,* and *PC Buying World* magazines.

About IDG Books Worldwide

Welcome to the world of IDG Books Worldwide.

IDG Books Worldwide, Inc., is a division of International Data Group, the world's largest publisher of computer-related information and the leading global provider of information services on information technology. IDG publishes over 194 computer publications in 62 countries. Forty million people read one or more IDG publications each month.

If you use personal computers, IDG Books is committed to publishing quality books that meet your needs. We rely on our extensive network of publications, including such leading periodicals as *Macworld, InfoWorld, PC World, Publish, Computerworld, Network World*, and *SunWorld*, to help us make informed and timely decisions in creating useful computer books that meet your needs.

Every IDG book strives to bring extra value and skill-building instruction to the reader. Our books are written by experts, with the backing of IDG periodicals, and with careful thought devoted to issues such as audience, interior design, use of icons, and illustrations. Our editorial staff is a careful mix of high-tech journalists and experienced book people. Our close contact with the makers of computer products helps ensure accuracy and thorough coverage. Our heavy use of personal computers at every step in production means we can deliver books in the most timely manner.

We are delivering books of high quality at competitive prices on topics customers want. At IDG, we believe in quality, and we have been delivering quality for over 25 years. You'll find no better book on a subject than an IDG book.

John Kilcullen
President and C.E.O.
IDG Books Worldwide, Inc.

IDG Books Worldwide, Inc. is a division of International Data Group. The officers are Patrick J. McGovern, Founder and Board Chairman; Walter Boyd, President. International Data Group's publications include: **ARGENTINA's** Computerworld Argentina, InfoWorld Argentina; **ASIA's** Computerworld Hong Kong, PC World Hong Kong, Computerworld Southeast Asia, PC World Singapore, Computerworld Malaysia, PC World Malaysia; **AUSTRALIA's** Computerworld Australia, Australian PC World, Australian Macworld, Network World, Reseller, IDG Sources; **AUSTRIA's** Computerwelt Oesterreich, PC Test; **BRAZIL's** Computerworld, Mundo IBM, Mundo Unix, PC World, Publish; **BULGARIA's** Computerworld Bulgaria, Ediworld, PC & Mac World Bulgaria; **CANADA's** Direct Access, Graduate Computerworld, InfoCanada, Network World Canada; **CHILE's** Computerworld, Informatica; **COLUMBIA's** Computerworld Columbia; **CZECH REPUBLIC's** Computerworld, Elektronika, PC World; **DENMARK's** CAD/CAM WORLD, Communications World, Computerworld Danmark, LOTUS World, Macintosh Produktkatalog, Macworld Danmark, PC World Danmark, PC World Produktguide, Windows World; **EQUADOR's** PC World; **EGYPT's** Computerworld (CW) Middle East, PC World Middle East; **FINLAND's** MikroPC, Tietoviikko, Tietoverkko; **FRANCE's** Distribuitique, GOLDEN MAC, InfoPC, Languages & Systems, Le Guide du Monde Informatique, Le Monde Informatique, Telecoms & Reseaux; **GERMANY's** Computerwoche, Computerwoche Focus, Computerwoche Extra, Computerwoche Karriere, Information Management, Macwelt, Netzwelt, PC Welt, PC Woche, Publish, Unit; **HUNGARY's** Alaplap, Computerworld SZT, PC World, ; **INDIA's** Computers & Communications; **ISRAEL's** Computerworld Israel, PC World Israel; **ITALY's** Computerworld Italia, Lotus Magazine, Macworld Italia, Networking Italia, PC World Italia; **JAPAN's** Computerworld Japan, Macworld Japan, SunWorld Japan, Windows World; **KENYA's** East African Computer News; **KOREA's** Computerworld Korea, Macworld Korea, PC World Korea; **MEXICO's** Compu Edicion, Compu Manufactura, Computacion/Punto de Venta, Computerworld Mexico, MacWorld, Mundo Unix, PC World, Windows; **THE NETHERLAND'S** Computer! Totaal, LAN Magazine, MacWorld; **NEW ZEALAND's** Computer Listings, Computerworld New Zealand, New Zealand PC World; **NIGERIA's** PC World Africa; **NORWAY's** Computerworld Norge, C/World, Lotusworld Norge, Macworld Norge, Networld, PC World Ekspress, PC World Norge, PC World's Product Guide, Publish World, Student Data, Unix World, Windowsworld, IDG Direct Response; **PANAMA's** PC World; **PERU's** Computerworld Peru, PC World; **PEOPLES REPUBLIC OF CHINA's** China Computerworld, PC World China, Electronics International, China Network World; **IDG HIGH TECH BEIJING's** New Product World; **IDG SHENZHEN's** Computer News Digest; **PHILLIPPINES'** Computerworld, PC World; **POLAND's** Computerworld Poland, PC World/ Komputer; **PORTUGAL's** Cerebro/PC World, Correio Informatico/Computerworld, MacIn; **ROMANIA's** PC World; **RUSSIA's** Computerworld-world, Mir-PC, Sety; **SLOVENIA's** Monitor Magazine; **SOUTH AFRICA's** Computing S.A.; **SPAIN's** Amiga World, Computerworld Espana, Communicaciones World, Macworld Espana, NeXTWORLD, PC World Espana, Publish, Sunworld; **SWEDEN's** Attack, ComputerSweden, Corporate Computing, Lokala Natverk/LAN, Lotus World, MAC&PC, Macworld, Mikrodatorn, PC World, Publishing & Design (CAP), Datalngenjoren, Maxi Data, Windows World; **SWITZERLAND's** Computerworld Schweiz, Macworld Schweiz, PC & Workstation; **TAIWAN's** Computerworld Taiwan, Global Computer Express, PC World Taiwan; **THAILAND's** Thai Computerworld; **TURKEY's** Computerworld Monitor, Macworld Turkiye, PC World Turkiye; **UNITED KINGDOM's** Lotus Magazine, Macworld, Sunworld; **UNITED STATES'** AmigaWorld, Cable in the Classroom, CD Review, CIO, Computerworld, Desktop Video World, DOS Resource Guide, Electronic News, Federal Computer Week, Federal Integrator, GamePro, IDG Books, InfoWorld, InfoWorld Direct, Laser Event, Macworld, Multimedia World, Network World, NeXTWORLD, PC Games, PC Letter, PC World Publish, Sumeria, SunWorld, SWATPro, Video Event; **VENEZUELA's** Computerworld Venezuela, MicroComputerworld Venezuela; **VIETNAM's** PC World Vietnam

Contents at a Glance

Preface

DOS For Dummies — and all the books in the *...For Dummies* series — are the ideal computer references. Have a problem? Great, look it up in *...For Dummies,* find out how to get it done right, and then close the book and return to your work. That's the way all computer books should work: quickly, painlessly, and with a dash of humor to keep the edge off.

So why is an Excel quick reference needed? Yikes! Who wants to look at that junk? Who cares about the Charts commands versus the Worksheet commands? Chances are you might, someday.

The way we work with computers is that we often imitate what others do. Fred may hand you a spreadsheet file and say, "Recalculate these formulas before you quit work today." Being suspicious—which is always good around Fred—you want to make sure you won't be doing anything disastrous. *Excel For Dummies* can't help you weasel out command formats and cryptic, seldom-used options on commands that are way beyond the reach of the typical Dummy. So what you're left with is the Excel manual or the fuzzy-headed on-line help.

Thank goodness for this book!

John Walkenbach has done the tedious job of transposing all the Excel commands from crypto-manual speak into a plain language reference we can use during those painful "must look it up in the manual" moments. He's peppered it with information, dos and don'ts, and the splash of humor you've come to expect from any book with *Dummies* on the title.

So tuck this reference in tight somewhere right by your PC. Keep it handy for when you must know the advanced options of some command or to confirm your worst fears about what it is Fred wants you to do to your own PC.

Dan Gookin

Introduction

Greetings. You're holding in your hands one of a different breed of computer reference books — a book written for normal people (not computer geeks). The *Excel For Dummies Quick Reference* is for those of you who have no aspirations to become a spreadsheet wizard. Rather, you want to be able to do your job efficiently so you can move on to more important things — like having a life.

This Book: Who Needs It?

I wrote this book for the hundreds of thousands of beginning to intermediate Excel users who have better things to do with their time than wade through technical dribble just to figure out how to do something.

When I was asked to write this book, I visited several local bookstores to get an idea of what I would be competing with for shelf space. I found dozens of Excel books and Excel command reference guides. With a few exceptions, these books are dull, boring, too technical, and not much fun to read. An exception to this state of affairs is Greg Harvey's *Excel For Dummies.* Because of its light-hearted approach to teaching about computers and software, the . . . *For Dummies* series is the most popular computer book series ever.

If you have absolutely no experience with Excel, *Excel For Dummies* is a better place to start. Actually, this book is designed to go hand in hand with Greg's book, so you'll probably want to own them both.

Why Another Excel Book?

Excel has always been the top-selling Windows spreadsheet. It has come a long way since it was first released in 1987, and most people who know about such things consider it to be the most powerful spreadsheet program available. Excel can be used at many different levels, and it's a safe bet that the majority of Excel users don't really have a clue as to what the program can really do when all the stops are pulled out. My goal is to open the door to some of the cool things that Excel can do — and do so in a way that doesn't put you to sleep.

On the one hand, Excel is very easy to use. I can spend 20 minutes with new users and have them doing semi-useful things by themselves after this initial session. But most Excel users eventually reach a head-scratching point in which they want to do something but can't figure out where the command is located. Or, they just can't seem to get a command to do what they think it *should* do.

Important Note: This book covers Excel for Windows Version 4.0. Although the book has value for Excel 3.0 users, the 4.0 upgrade added lots of new features that aren't in Excel 3. By the way, if you use Excel for the Macintosh Version 4.0, you'll find that most of the commands are identical across the Mac version and the Windows version.

Mousing Around

Some day, computers will be able to respond to your vocal commands. You could say something like, "Hey computer, run Excel and load that file I was working on Thursday afternoon. Then change the interest rate cell to 8.5 percent. Thanks, dude." Until that day arrives, you're going to have to give commands in a way that the computer can understand.

If you have used Excel for even a few minutes, you undoubtedly know that clicking the menu bar opens the door to a staggering number of commands by displaying drop-down menus. You can change how your numbers look, move stuff around, print your work, and even perform an analysis of variance if you're so moved.

The truth of the matter is that virtually no one actually needs or uses *all* the Excel commands. Most users get by just fine after they learn the basics. But if you stick to the basics, you run the risk of causing more work for yourself. For example, Excel has commands that automate operations that may take you an hour to do manually. Saving 10 minutes here or a half hour there adds up over time. You'll have more time for fun things and can maybe even get out of the office at a reasonable hour — not to mention the fact that people will be amazed at how efficient you have become.

How the Commands Look

Because this reference guide is all about the Excel commands, we need to be on the same wavelength. In other words, you need to know where my head was at when I was writing all this stuff and nonsense.

Most of this book consists of discussion of Excel's commands. Here's an example using the File⇨Open command. As you may already know, this particular command brings up a dialog box that lets you choose a file to work on. When I talk about this command later on in the book, it'll appear in the heading as:

File⇨Open...

The icons that appear with each command name tell you at a glance something about the command — how often you are likely to use it and how safe it is for you to use.

Because the command name is followed by three dots (officially known as an *ellipsis*), you know right off the bat that issuing this command gives you a dialog box. Each command starts out with a brief English-language description of what it does. Then I tell you why you would ever want (or need) to use this command and provide an overview of how to use it. If there's anything else you should know about, you'll find it here. Finally, I refer you to other commands that may be of interest — one of them could be the one that you *really* want to use.

Parts IV, V, and VI are organized in lists and tables to give you easy access to the information they offer you.

What the Little Pictures Mean

All the good computer books have little icons sprinkled liberally throughout their pages. These icons work great for visually oriented people and tell you in an instant a few key things about each command. Hoping that icons really work for you, I've inserted plenty of them. Here's what the icons in this book mean.

This icon flags commands that are used by almost all Excel users. It's probably worth your while to learn about this command.

This icon flags commands that are generally not used by beginners, although you might have a use for them.

This icon flags commands that are normally used only by advanced Excel users or for special purposes. These commands can be useful at times.

This icon flags commands that are safe for your data.

This icon flags commands that are generally safe in most circumstances unless you really don't follow instructions; then look out.

This icon flags commands that are potentially dangerous to data but necessary in the scheme of things. Be very careful when you use this command!

This icon flags a command that is available only if you've loaded a particular add-in file.

 This icon flags a command (or part of it) that is available as an icon on a toolbar.

 This icon flags problem areas that can mess up your work if you're not on your toes.

 This icon flags a way of using the command that may not be immediately obvious to the average bear.

 This icon flags something that you should store away in the deep recesses of your cortex.

 This icon flags cross references to other areas of this book that might be of interest.

 This icon flags material that tells you where to look in *Excel For Dummies* for more information. If (for some unknown reason) you don't have *Excel For Dummies,* don't bother reading this stuff.

How You Can Use This Book

You can use this book in several ways.

- If you need to find out how to do something in Excel, look up the main menu command (they're listed in alphabetical order within the two main parts of the book, not the order in which they appear on-screen). Browse through the discussion until you find something that looks relevant and then read it.

- If you don't have a clue as to the proper command to look up, head for the index and look at words that describe what you want to do. This usually steers you to the command that you're looking for.

- If you need to find out why something isn't working the way you think it should, look up the command and read about it. I throw in all sorts of useful tips and techniques at no extra charge.

- If you find yourself with a spare hour or two while circling over LAX waiting to land, browse through it and read things that are interesting to you. If you find that nothing in this book passes that criterion, you're not alone. However, if you continue to page through the book, you just might discover something that you didn't know Excel could do — and it just might be what you need for a project you're working on.

- Keep it lying around on your desk. That way, people walking by will stop and make idle conversation while trying to get a look at the book without actually telling you they need the help! It's a good way to kill some time when you should be working.

How Not to Use This Book: Whatever you do, don't read this book from cover to cover. Frankly, the plot stinks, the character development leaves much to be desired, and you'll be disappointed by the ending. Although it's moderately entertaining, the book is not exactly what you would call a page-turner!

How I Organized This Book

This book is divided into six parts.

Part I: A Crash Course in Excel. This section is a quick and dirty overview of Excel basics. I was tempted to leave this information out and simply refer you to *Excel For Dummies,* but I'm a nice guy.

Part II: The Excel Worksheet Command Reference. Here's the heart of the book, as it were. It's an alphabetical listing of all the menu commands available in the Worksheet window — with just enough detail for most people.

Part III: The Excel Chart Command Reference. If Part II is the heart of the book, this section is more like the liver. This section is where you find the commands that are relevant when you're working on a chart in a Chart Window.

Part IV: The Dummies Guide to Excel's Toolbars. You can save yourself lots of time and effort by using the toolbars provided with Excel. But you need to know what the tools do and when to use them. Here's where to find the scoop on toolbar icons.

Part V: The Dummies Guide to Excel's Worksheet Functions. All those weird — but sometimes useful — functions are described here in language that you can understand.

Part VI: The Dummies Guide to Excel's Keyboard Commands. For one reason or another, some people prefer to use a mouse whenever possible. The fact is, you can often do things more quickly by using the keyboard. If doing things at warp speed appeals to you, read through this section to become familiar with the gajillion or so Excel keyboard commands at your disposal.

With that out of the way, let's move on to some actual substance.

6

Part 1:
A Crash Course in Excel

For those of you who haven't yet treated yourselves to *Excel For Dummies*, here's the condensed version (but with no "Humor in Uniform section"). You can read through this section to get a quick overview of Excel or use it to refresh those brain cells that have lost their charge. Be warned, however, that this section is by no means conclusive. In other words, I left out lots of tidbits that are explained more thoroughly in *Excel For Dummies*.

Basic Excel Knowledge

Excel is one of several spreadsheet programs that software
vendors try to get you to buy. Other spreadsheets that you may
have heard of included Lotus 1-2-3, Borland's Quattro Pro, and
Computer Associates' SuperCalc. Many others have come and
gone over the years, but these are by far the most popular ones.

A *spreadsheet program* essentially lets you work with numbers
and words in a large grid of cells. The grid of cells that you work
with is called a *worksheet* (because it is an on-screen version of an
accountant's worksheet), and every worksheet is stored in a file
with an XLS extension. Excel, like all other spreadsheets, can also
create graphs from numbers stored in a worksheet and work with
database information stored in a record and field format.

Every Excel worksheet has 16,384 rows and 256 columns. *Rows*
are numbered from 1 to 16,384, and *columns* are labeled with
letters. Column 1 is A, column 26 is Z, column 27 is AA, column 52
is AZ, column 53 is BZ, and so on up to column 256 (which is IV).

The intersection of a row and column is called a *cell*. My calcula-
tor tells me that this works out to 4,194,304 cells — which should
be enough cells for most people. Actually, you would run out of
memory long before you even come *close* to using all the cells.
Cells have addresses, which are based on the row and column
that they are in. The upper left cell in a worksheet is called *A1,*
and the cell way down at the bottom is called *IV256.* Cell K9 (also
known as the dog cell) is the intersection of the eleventh column
and the ninth row.

A cell in Excel can hold a number, some text, a formula, or
nothing at all. A *formula* is a special way to tell Excel to perform a
calculation using information stored in other cells. For example,
you can insert a formula that tells Excel to add up the values in
the first 10 cells in column A and display the result in the cell that
has the formula. Formulas can use normal arithmetic operators
such as + (plus), - (minus), * (multiply), and / (divide). They can
also use special built-in functions that let you do powerful things
without much effort on your part. For example, Excel has functions that add up a range of values, calculate square roots,
compute loan payments, and even tell you the time of day.

The Active Cell and Ranges

When you issue a command, it works on the *active cell* or the
selected range. In Excel, one of the 4 million and some odd cells is
always the active cell and the commands you issue work on this
cell alone. A group of cells, or the selected range, can also act as
an active cell, in which case, the commands you issue work on all
the cells in the selected range.

You can select a range by clicking and dragging the mouse over the cells that you want to include. The selected range is usually a group of contiguous cells, but the cells don't have to be consecutive. If you press and hold the Ctrl key each time you press the mouse button and drag the mouse to select a range, you can select more than one group of cells. Then the commands you issue will work on all of the selected cells.

You can select continuous and discontinuous ranges with the keyboard, too, although not in as carefree a manner as with the mouse. For one contiguous range selection, press and hold Shift (or press F8) and then use the direction keys to highlight all the cells you want in the range. If you need nonadjacent selections in the range, press F8 and use the direction keys, press Shift+F8 and move the cursor to the anchor cell in the next location, and then press F8 and select the next part of the range.

Just about anything you do with a mouse in Excel, you can also do using just the keyboard. The only exception is using the icons on the toolbars — you need a mouse for those operations.

Navigational Techniques

With more than 4 million cells in a worksheet, you need ways to move to specific cells. Fortunately, Excel provides you with many techniques to move around through a worksheet. As always, you can use either your mouse or the keyboard on your navigational journeys. The navigational keys are covered in Part 6.

The Excel Screen

This figure shows a typical Excel screen, with some of the important parts pointed out. This terminology rears its ugly head throughout this book, so pay attention.

Formula bar
Standard toolbox
Control-menu box
Title bar
Menu bar
Restore button
Minimize button

Status bar
Document window

Filling up the Cells

A cell can hold a number (value), a text entry (label), a formula, or nothing at all. If you want to put a number in a cell, just start typing it and press Enter when you're done. Then move to another cell and do it again.

To put text in a cell, just start typing it and press Enter when you're done. You can put a lot of text in a cell — much more than you might think, given the width of a typical cell. If the cell to the right is empty, the text appears to "spill over" into it. If the neighboring cell is not empty, the text gets cut off on-screen if it's wider than the column (it's all there, it just doesn't show).

Entering formulas is another story. Usually, formulas refer to other cells and use their values. Here's a simple formula:

```
=(A1+A2)/2
```

This formula adds the values (numbers) in cells A1 and A2 and divides the result by 2. Cells A1 and A2 can hold either numbers or other formulas. If either of these cells has a label (text), Excel interprets it as zero. Whenever either cell A1 or A2 changes, the formula displays a new answer.

Giving Commands to Excel

To do the things that spreadsheet users do, you have to use the Excel commands. Here's a typical Excel command:

File⇨Open

This command is used to read a worksheet file into Excel so that you can work on it. You can invoke this command in several different ways:

1. Click on the File menu with the mouse and then click on the Open command.

2. Press Alt+F (for File) and then O (for Open).

3. Press Alt or the F10 key to activate the menu bar. Use the arrow keys to move to the File menu and press Enter. Then, use the arrow keys to move to the Open command and press Enter again to issue the command.

4. Click on the icon on the toolbar that looks like an opening folder.

5. Press Ctrl+F12 (or Alt+Ctrl+F2 if your keyboard lacks the F12 key).

All these techniques lead to the end result of the File Open dialog box, which you use to tell Excel which file you want to open. After the dialog box appears, you can use your mouse or keyboard to carry on the dialog and tell Excel what you're trying to do.

Even though having all these command-issuing options available may seem a bit confusing, you don't have to learn them all. Most people simply learn one method and stick to it. Also, not all commands have so many options. Because the File⇨Open command is used so frequently, Excel designers went overboard and came up with several ways to do it.

Most commands lead to a dialog box, but some commands do their thing immediately with no additional work required on your part. You can tell the commands that lead to a dialog box because they are followed by ellipses (...) in the drop-down menu.

Yet another way to issue commands in Excel involves the mouse again. If you click on objects, an individual cell, or a selected range of cells by using the *right* mouse button, Excel displays a context-sensitive menu which lists common commands that are appropriate to the element you clicked on.

Working with Dialog Boxes

Excel, like virtually every other Windows application, is big on dialog boxes. A *dialog box* is a small window that pops up in response to most of the commands that you issue. This window appears right on top of what you're doing in the worksheet— a sure sign that you must make some type of response to the dialog box before you can do anything else.

This figure shows a typical Excel dialog box. This particular dialog box is displayed when you select the File⇨Page Setup command. I chose this for an example because it contains many (but not all) of the types of dialog box controls that you're likely to encounter.

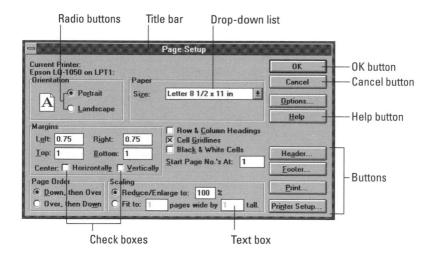

Dialog box parts

Here's a fairly exhaustive list of the various controls and other parts you'll be up against in the world of dialog boxes.

Title bar: The colored bar at the top of the dialog box. Click and drag this bar to move the dialog box to a different part of the screen if it's covering up something you want to see.

Radio buttons: Round buttons, usually enclosed in a group box. Only one radio button can be "on" at a time. When you choose a radio button, the others in the group are turned off — just as on an old-fashioned car radio.

Drop-down list: A list of things you can choose from. These lists have a small arrow that points downward. Click on the arrow to drop the list down.

Text box: A box in which you enter something — a number or text.

Check box: A square box that you can select to turn the option on or off.

List box: A box that shows several items to choose from and that usually has a vertical scroll bar that you can use to display more items in the list (you can't see a list box in this dialog box figure).

OK button: The button you choose when you have made your dialog box selections and want to get on with it.

Cancel button: The button you choose when you change your mind. None of the changes you made to the dialog box take effect.

Help button: The button you choose to display Excel's on-line help system about the dialog box you're working in.

Button: A dialog box button you choose in order to do something else. If the text in the button has three dots after it, choosing that button brings up another dialog box.

Navigating through dialog boxes

You can work with a dialog box by using your mouse or the keyboard. The choice is yours.

If you use a mouse, simply position the mouse cursor on the option you want to work with and click. The exact procedure varies with the type of control, but the good news is that all Windows programs work the same way. If you learn to use Excel dialog boxes, you have a head start when you try to learn another Windows program. And if you already use other Windows programs, you will feel right at home with Excel's dialog boxes.

You'll notice that the various parts of a dialog box are named with words or phrases that contain a single underlined letter. You can use that letter in combination with the Alt key to jump to that part of the dialog box. For example, in the Page Setup dialog box, you can quickly select the Paper Size drop-down list by pressing Alt+Z. Besides using Alt+key combinations, you can use Tab and Shift+Tab to cycle through all the controls in a dialog box.

Mousing Around with Toolbars

One of the greatest timesaving features in Excel is its toolbars. Excel comes with ten toolbars, each of which has a bunch of icons that provide shortcuts for commonly used commands and procedures. You can, for example, click on the icon that left-aligns the contents of a cell or range *much* faster than issuing the Format⇒Alignment command and then making your selection in the dialog box. In other words, it's well worth your effort to learn about the toolbars. Your opportunity to do so comes up in Part IV.

Actually Doing Things with Excel

The process of using Excel involves entering data and formulas into cells, manipulating the data in various ways using the menu commands and dialog boxes, and then printing the results on paper for the rest of the world to enjoy. And if you're smart, you'll take advantage of the toolbar icons and shortcut keys to make the process even easier. Not coincidentally, all these things are covered in the rest of this book.

Part II:
The Excel Worksheet Command Reference

OK folks, here's the good stuff, the reason you laid your good money on the counter for this information-packed little book.

The following pages explain every single Excel worksheet command that you can possibly give. I'll be the first to admit that I provide longer explanations for the more commonly used commands — but that's probably why you chose this book in the first place, right? If, however, you're ever held at gunpoint and ordered to insert an OLE object into a worksheet, you can rest assured that you can find out what it's all about by venturing no further than the book you now hold in your hands.

If you find that some of the commands listed here don't show up on your menu, that's because the command is enabled by loading an add-in file. All these add-in commands are identified by an icon. To make the command available, first load the add-in file, which is probably located in your \EXCEL\LIBRARY directory. If you need to use a particular add-in command frequently, consider making it load automatically with the Options⇨Add-ins command. If your \EXCEL\LIBRARY directory is empty or doesn't exist, run Excel's Setup program and tell it that you want to install the macro library.

Data Menu Commands

This menu is where it's happening when you're working with a *spreadsheet database* — an organized collection of information arranged by records (rows) and fields (columns). It also houses the commands to sort cells and ranges and do lots of other things that are best described as advanced.

Excel databases is the topic of Chapter 8 in *Excel For Dummies.*

Data⇨Consolidate...

Lets you combine corresponding cells from different ranges or different worksheets — and does so "intelligently" by matching row and column titles.

If you're in charge of your company's budget and need to consolidate individual departmental budgets into a master corporate budget, this command can save you hours of manual labor. The command's usefulness extends beyond budgeting; it is handy for all sorts of consolidation chores.

How you use it

First, make sure that all the worksheets to be consolidated (the source documents) are available and that the ranges to be consolidated are all set up identically (or at least use the same row and column headers). Issue the Data⇨Consolidate command and fill in the dialog box, specifying the references in each worksheet to the list.

The section entitled "Consolidate your holdings" in Chapter 9 of *Excel For Dummies* explains this process in detail.

If you use the option to match row and column labels, be aware that the labels must match *exactly* for Excel to consider them the same. For example, *Oct* does not match up with *October.*

More stuff

Besides summing the corresponding values, you can choose from a variety of other mathematical operations in the Function drop-down list in the Consolidate dialog box.

If you choose the box labeled Create Links to Source Data, Excel creates formulas that use external references. If you don't know what you're doing, these links can be very confusing, but, with them, the consolidation is automatic if any of the data in the worksheets you're consolidating get changed.

Data⇨Crosstab...

Summarizes a database practically any way you want by creating a handy table.

This add-in is installed automatically when you install Excel and is loaded when you choose the Data⇨Crosstab command.

If you have a lot of data in a spreadsheet database, you'll eventually need to summarize it in some way. For example, if you're the personnel director for a company that keeps its employee records in an Excel database, you could produce a report that shows the number of employees categorized by date hired and by salary level (assuming, of course, that this information is kept in the database).

How you use it

After you've defined your database, choose the Data⇨Crosstab command and then follow the directions in the Crosstab Wizard dialog boxes.

If you just want to get a quick and dirty record count from a database, setting up a criteria range to specify what you want to count and then using one of the database functions (such as =DCOUNT) to give you the answer you want may be easier and faster.

Data⇨Delete

Removes records from an Excel database that meet criteria you specify in the criteria range. It also moves the other records up to fill in the holes. Using this command is a fast way to nuke database records that you no longer need.

How you use it

Let's say you need to remove all records in a database that have the word *Paid* in the Status field. You can set up a criteria range that selects records that you want and then issue this command. In a snap, all paid-up customer records are eliminated from your database — much faster than scrolling through and doing it manually one at a time (yuk!).

Save your file before using this command. The Edit⇨Undo command cannot bring deleted records back from the dead.

Data⇨Set Criteria, Data⇨Set Database

Data⇨Extract...

Copies records that meet your criteria (specified in the criteria range) from an Excel database to your extract range. This command is useful if you want to do something with only a subset of the records in your database. For example, you might want to send a memo only to people who live in Tulsa. This command can extract only those records; then you can use them in conjunction with your word processor's mail merge feature. You can also create a new database from an existing one with this command. Simply extract the records that you want to go into the new database and save them in a separate worksheet.

Excel overwrites any data that gets in the way while it's extracting, so it's best to make sure there's nothing below the headings at the top of the extract range. Better yet, save your file beforehand because Edit⇨Undo won't come to your rescue after you use this command.

More stuff

Before you can use this command, you need to identify your database and set up a criteria range and an extract range.

If you want to limit the extracted data to a specific number of records, make the extract range extend down below the field names to include the number of records you want. When the extract range is filled, Excel stops extracting.

The dialog box for this command has an option called Unique Records Only. If you check this box, the extracted data include no duplicates. This is a good way to weed out duplicate records in a database.

Data⇨Set Criteria, Data⇨Set Database, Data⇨Set Extract

Data⇨Find

Locates records in an Excel database that meet the criteria you specify in the criteria range. Using this command is a quick way to browse through specific records in a database, without extracting them to a separate extract range.

How you use it

First, you must define your database and set up a criterion range. Then, when you choose Data⇨Find, Excel highlights the first record that meets your criteria. You can then use the arrow keys to move to other records that meet the criteria. To get out of this mode, choose Data⇨Exit Find or just click anywhere outside of the database.

More stuff

You can also use the Data⇨Form command to browse through records that meet simple criteria.

Data⇨Set Criteria, Data⇨Set Database, Data⇨Form, Formula⇨Find

---

Data⇨Exit Find

Stops finding records. Using this command is one way to cancel the Data⇨Find command. You can also just click somewhere outside the database.

More stuff

This command is available only while you're finding records.

Data⇨Find

Data⇨Form...

Displays a handy form that makes entering data into an Excel database, browsing through a database, or locating or deleting records that meet simple criteria easier.

Many people find that doing routine database entry using a form is easier than entering the stuff directly into the worksheet. Using this command is also a handy way to view database records. You can use this command in place of many of the normal Data commands.

How you use it

First, define your database. Then, when you issue the Data⇨Form command, Excel displays a form that shows all your database fields, listed vertically. You can use the vertical scrollbar to scroll though the records.

More stuff

The dialog box that pops up when you choose the Data⇨Form command has lots of buttons on it. You can add a new record (the database definition is extended automatically to include the new arrival), delete the displayed record, and enter simple search criteria to limit the records displayed.

Excel For Dummies explains all this stuff more thoroughly in the section entitled "Data in What Form?" in Chapter 8.

Data⇨Set Database

Data⇨Parse...

Converts long strings of text into their component parts and puts the parts into separate columns.

As you may know, Excel can read in text files, which are often produced by other programs. But when Excel reads in a text file, it simply stores the entire file in a single column. Usually, you want the various parts of each line to show up in separate columns. The Data⇨Parse command can do this for you in a snap.

How you use it

First, have Excel read in the text file that you want using the File⇨Open command. Although the file may look pretty good on-screen, careful examination reveals that everything is actually stored in the first column. Select the entire column and then choose the Data⇨Parse command. In the dialog box that appears, choose Guess to let Excel guess how to break the strings into pieces. It inserts brackets that represent where the column breaks will occur. Choose OK and see if it worked correctly. If not, choose Edit⇨Undo, adjust the brackets in the guess line manually, and try again.

Excel remembers the previous parse line, so you may want to move the cell pointer to a row that's most typical of the others and let Excel take its guess on that line. Then, select all the other data using the previous guess.

More stuff

By default, Excel overwrites the original data with the parsed data. You can specify a different destination, if you like. This new location keeps the original imported stuff from being replaced with the new parsed stuff.

Data⇨Smart Parse

Data⇨Series...

Fills a range of cells with numbers or words in a series. You control the start value, stop value, and increment value. Using this command is a fast way to fill up a range with numbers, dates, times, or even words such as month or day names.

The AutoFill feature is a faster way of accomplishing the same thing.

How you use it

There are lots of options available in the Series dialog box. Choose the Help button for more information.

If the range you select prior to issuing this command has data in it, the contents are replaced with new data without warning.

Data⇨Set Criteria

When working with a database, tells Excel where your criteria range is stored. If you're planning on using Data⇨Find, Data⇨Extract, or Data⇨Delete, you must set a criteria range first.

How you use it

Usually, copying the field names from the first row of the database to another area is easiest. Then, select the copied cells along with the number of rows below that you need (usually, one extra row is enough). Issue the Data⇨Set Criteria command to tell Excel where it is.

After you choose Data⇨Set Criteria, Excel creates a range name for it called *criteria.* You can use the Formula⇨Define Name command to adjust the criteria range after the fact.

More stuff

The criteria range doesn't have to include all the fields from the database. In fact, it can consist of as few as one field.

Data⇨Set Database

Data⇨Set Database

Tells Excel where the database is located on your worksheet. This information is necessary when performing procedures on an Excel database. If you plan on doing anything like extracting data, finding data, or deleting data from a database, you must first define the database.

How you use it

Make sure the first row contains field names. Simply choose the field names and all the rows of data below (plus one blank row at the bottom) and then choose the Data⇨Set Database command.

After you choose Data⇨Set Database, Excel creates a range name for it called *database*. You can use the Formula⇨Define Name command to adjust the database range after the fact. You can also use the F5 (Goto) key to display a list of range names. Choose database to select the entire database.

Although a single worksheet can hold any number of databases, only one of them at time can be the "official" database. So if your worksheet has more than one database, make sure that you're really working with the one you think you're working with.

Data⇨Set Criteria

Data⇨Set Extract

Tells Excel where the extract range is on your worksheet. Using this command is a necessary step before you use the Data⇨Extract command to extract data from an Excel database.

How you use it

Copy the field names from the first row of your database into another area of the worksheet and make sure there's plenty of room below to hold the extracted records. Select the copied field names and enough rows below it to hold the data that you are extracting. Issue the Data⇨Set Extract command to tell Excel where you want the records to go.

More stuff

Excel creates a range named *extract* that corresponds to the extract range you specify.

If you don't know how many records you are extracting, you can select only the row with the field names to create an "unlimited" extract range.

If your extract range consists of only the row with the field names, Excel erases everything below, even if it doesn't get in the way of the extracted data. In other words, if you choose an unlimited extract range, make sure that there's nothing else in the cells below. The Edit⇨Undo command cannot help out if you screw up.

Data⇨Extract

Data⇨Smart Parse...

Lets you break up text strings into their component parts and put them into separate columns.

This command is not available unless you load the FLATFILE.XLA add-in file.

This command is useful if you import an ASCII file that has its parts delimited by a specific character (such as a semicolon). Using this command can quickly separate the parts of the text.

How you use it

Select the cells to be parsed and choose Data⇨Smart Parse. Excel displays a dialog box that lets you specify that delimiter. Choose OK, and the text is broken apart, with each part in a separate column.

Data⇨Parse

Data⇨Sort...

Rearranges a range of cells into ascending or descending order, using one or more rows or columns as a sorting key. You may want to sort data for many reasons: to make finding things easier, to present results from best to worst, to alphabetize a list, to sort entries by date, and so on.

How you use it

First, select the entire range that you want to sort. Issue the Data⇨Sort command. In the Sort dialog box, choose either Rows or Columns (Rows is the most common choice). Choose the box that's labeled 1st Key and then click *anywhere* in the column (or row) that you want to do the sorting on. Choose OK to do the sort.

When you're sorting a range that includes more than one column (such as a database), make double-sure that you choose everything that you want to sort — not just one column. Otherwise, the records in your database will be completely scrambled. If you discover that you screwed up, choose Edit⇨Undo immediately to restore the range to its presorted order. To be on the safe side, save your file before you do any major sorting.

More stuff

You can specify two additional sort keys, if necessary. Using more than one sort key is how you handle ties. For example, in a name and address database, you might want to sort by last name (1st Key). But what if multiple people have the same last name? In this case, you would probably want to specify first name as the 2nd Key. That way, the data are sorted by last name and by first name when there are multiple records with the same last name.

You can learn even more about sorting by consulting *Excel For Dummies* in the section entitled "Data from A to Z (or 'So, Sort Me!')" in Chapter 8.

Data⇨Table...

Creates a table that shows how specific cells in your worksheet change when another cell or cells are changed. Some worksheets are set up with formulas that allow you to ask "what if" questions. For example, *What if we raise prices by 5 percent?*, or *What if I get fired next week?* This command can summarize the results of a bunch of what-if scenarios in the form of a nicely formatted table.

How you use it

This command is a pretty advanced, and explaining it would take several pages to do it justice. Frankly, using Excel's Scenario Manager is a much better way to go.

Formula⇨Scenario Manager

Edit Menu Commands

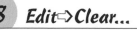

Commands on this menu let you manipulate cells and ranges. Several of these commands use the Windows Clipboard, which is a way to copy information between different Windows applications. It also has some other commands that deal with copying and other issues.

Edit⇨Clear...

Clears everything from a cell or range. Optionally, you can clear only the formats, only the formulas, or only the attached notes. When you want to get rid of the stuff in a cell or range, this is the way to go. It's also a handy way to get rid of a cell's formatting, without nuking the contents of the cell.

How you use it

Select the cell or range that you want to clear and then choose the Edit⇨Clear command. In the Clear dialog box, choose what you want to clear out.

Don't confuse this command with the Edit⇨Delete command, which not only clears the cells but also removes them (and shifts the other cells around to accommodate their removal).

A common error people make is using the spacebar to "delete" the contents of a cell. Actually, the spacebar places a character in the cell — which happens to be invisible, so it looks as if the cell is empty. The fact is that this habit can cause you major problems, which are difficult to diagnose. So take my advice and don't erase cells with the spacebar. Thanks.

More stuff

Pressing Delete also brings up the Clear dialog box, which appears with the Formulas radio button selected as a default, not the All radio button.

You can also erase cells using Excel's drag and drop technique. Select the range that you want to erase and drag the fill handle up or left. The cells that you drag over have a shaded pattern on them. Release the mouse button, and all the shaded cells are erased.

Edit⇨Delete

Edit⇨Copy

Copies whatever is selected to the Windows Clipboard. This material can then be pasted into another location in an Excel worksheet or even into another Windows application. This command is commonly used, and you won't get too far without it.

How you use it

First, select the cell or range that you want to copy. Choose the Edit⇨Copy command. Excel displays a moving "marquee" around the selection and a message at the bottom of the screen asking you to choose the destination and either press Enter or choose Edit⇨Paste. If you move the cell pointer to a new location and press Enter, Excel pastes the copied cells to the new cell pointer position. If you move the cell pointer to a new location and choose Edit⇨Paste, Excel pastes the copied cells there and *leaves it on the Clipboard* so you can paste it somewhere else.

If you want to make multiple copies of a cell or range, use Edit⇨Copy, followed by Edit⇨Paste (multiple times).

If you attempt to copy to a location that already contains information, Excel overwrites the information that is already there without warning.

More stuff

You can also use this command to copy text from the formula bar. If you're creating a formula that's similar to one that already exists, you can steal the relevant part of the formula from the existing formula by copying it. Then, use Edit⇨Paste at the appropriate place in the formula you're creating.

If you're copying something to neighboring cells, you might prefer to do the copying simply by dragging the AutoFill handle on the cell or range that you're copying.

If you're simply copying from one cell to the cell below, use Ctrl+' (single quote) to copy the formula from the cell above or Ctrl+Shift+' (single quote) to copy the value from the cell above. Also, if you select a range before you enter a formula, you can use Ctrl+Enter to put the formula into all cells in the selection in one fell swoop (saving you from copying it later).

Ctrl+C is a shortcut for this command.

Edit⇨Cut, Edit⇨Paste, Edit⇨Fill Down, Edit⇨Fill Right

Edit⇨Copy Picture

Copies an image of the selection to the Windows Clipboard, so you can use it as a graphic. The image also includes the row and column borders. **Note:** This command appears only if you hold down Shift while you choose the Edit command.

This command might be handy if you want to include part of your worksheet in a graphics program, or if you need to show part of an Excel worksheet in a training manual produced with a word processor.

More stuff

The picture that you copy is not linked to the original cells. To create a linked picture, use the camera tool on the Utility toolbar.

How you use it

Select a cell or cells, hold down Shift, and then choose Edit⇨Copy Picture. Excel responds with a dialog box in which you can choose some options. Usually, the default settings are fine. Choose OK to copy a pictorial representation of the selection to the Clipboard.

Camera tool on the Utility toolbar, Edit⇨Paste Picture

Edit⇨Cut

Cuts (or deletes) whatever is selected and puts it on the Windows Clipboard. The selection can then be pasted into another location in an Excel worksheet or into another Windows application. Using this command is the way to move a cell or range from one place to another.

How you use it

First, select the cell or range that you want to cut. Choose the Edit⇨Cut command. Excel displays a moving *marquee* around the selection and a message at the bottom of the screen asking you to select the destination and either press Enter or choose Edit⇨Paste. If you move the cell cursor to the new location and press Enter, Excel pastes the cut cells to the new cell pointer position.

If you move to a new location and choose Edit⇨Paste, Excel pastes the copied cells there but *does not* leave it on the Clipboard (so you can't paste it again somewhere else). Note that this command differs from how pasting works when you copy stuff with the Edit⇨Copy command.

Be careful that you don't confuse this command with Edit⇨Delete or Edit⇨Clear — both of which remove stuff from cells, not move it to the Clipboard.

If you attempt to move a cell or range to a location that already contains information, Excel overwrites the information that is already there without warning.

More stuff

Ctrl+X is a shortcut for this command.

Edit⇨Copy, Edit⇨Paste, Edit⇨Delete, Edit⇨Clear

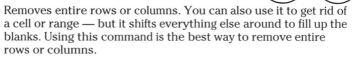
Edit⇨Delete...

Removes entire rows or columns. You can also use it to get rid of a cell or range — but it shifts everything else around to fill up the blanks. Using this command is the best way to remove entire rows or columns.

How you use it

Select the cell, range, row(s), or column(s) you want to get rid of and then choose the Edit⇨Delete command. If the selection is a cell or range, Excel displays a dialog box that asks you how you want to shift the other cells around to fill up the hole. Otherwise, it zaps the selection. If you delete rows, it shifts all the other rows up. If you delete columns, it shifts the other columns to the left.

Be careful when you use this command on a single cell or a range. Shifting other cells around can cause other parts of your worksheet to get messed up — and you may not even realize it until later.

Edit⇨Clear

Edit⇨Fill Down

Copies the first cell (or top row of cells) in a range to all the other cells below it in the selection.

If you hold down Shift when you choose the Edit menu, this command reads Fill Up. Using this command is one way to copy a cell or range to an adjacent cell or range quickly. You might find that Excel's AutoFill feature is more efficient for quick copying.

How you use it

Start your selection at the cell or single-row range you want to copy and then extend the selection down to include all the cells you want to copy it to. Choose Edit⇨Fill Do_w_n, and voilà — it's copied.

If the cells in the range you're copying to aren't empty, Excel overwrites them without warning.

Edit⇨Fill Right

Edit⇨Fill Group...

Copies a cell or range from the active worksheet to all others in the workgroup when you have multiple worksheets in a workgroup. Using this command is the express route to putting the same information in several different worksheets. It's particularly useful for filling in row and column headings or formulas. Another use is to copy just the formatting from one sheet to several others.

How you use it

First, make sure that all the worksheets are open and are defined as a workgroup with the Options⇨Group Edit command. Select the cell or range you want to copy and choose Edit⇨Fill Group. Excel pops up a dialog box that asks you what you want to copy — everything, just the formats, or just the contents. Make your choice and choose OK.

If the other worksheets have information in the corresponding cells, the information that is already there is replaced without warning.

Options⇨Group Edit

Edit⇨Fill Right

Copies the first cell (or left column of cells) in a range to all the other cells to the right of it in the selection.

If you hold down Shift when you choose the Edit menu, this command reads Fill Left.

Using this command is one way to copy a cell or range to an adjacent cell or range quickly. You might find that Excel's AutoFill feature is more efficient for this.

How you use it

Start your selection at the cell or single-column range you want to copy and then extend the selection to the right to include all the cells you want to copy it to. Choose Edit⇨Fill Right, and the cell or range is copied.

If the cells in the range you're copying to aren't empty, Excel overwrites them without warning.

Edit⇨Fill Down

Edit⇨Glossary...

Saves commonly used cells or formulas so you can quickly insert them.

This command does not appear unless the GLOSSARY.XLA add-in file has been loaded.

Using this command can be a good alternative to simple macros. If you find that you tend to put the same stuff into different cells, you can create a glossary entry that consists of this information and give it a name. Then, you can insert the same stuff by clicking a glossary name.

How you use it

Start by creating what you want to be in the glossary. Your glossary entry can be a single cell or a range and can hold values, text, or formulas. Select the cells, choose Edit⇨Glossary, and enter a meaningful name in the Name box. Then choose the Define button. When you want to insert this glossary later, choose Edit⇨Glossary and double-click on the name you gave it or choose the Insert button.

More stuff

The glossary entries are stored directly in the GLOSSARY.XLA file, which is updated with your new entries when you exit Excel.

Edit⇨Insert...

Lets you insert new rows, new columns, or a new cell or range of cells. If you insert a new cell or range, you must tell Excel how you want to shift the other cells around to make room. Using this command is an easy way to make room for new stuff that you forgot about and eliminates the need to move things out of the way.

How you use it

If you're inserting rows or columns, select entire rows or columns by clicking on the border. Choose the Edit⇨Insert command to make the insertion. For example, if you select five columns before issuing this command, Excel inserts five *new* columns and moves everything to the right. If you insert new rows, all the other rows are shifted down.

If you're inserting a cell or range, select the cell or range where you want the insertion to be and then issue the command. Excel responds with a dialog box that asks you how you want to shift the cell.

Be careful when inserting a cell or range since shifting cells around can cause problems elsewhere in the worksheet.

Edit⇨Insert Object...

Lets you insert an OLE object into a worksheet. OLE stands for Object Linking and Embedding, and an OLE object can be a drawing, a document, or many other types of things.

Using this command is one way to put information from other Windows applications into a worksheet — and let you use the tools in the other application to create and edit it. For example, you can insert a drawing from the Windows Paintbrush program directly into a worksheet.

How you use it

Choose the Edit⇨Insert Object command, and Excel displays a dialog box that lists all the possible sources that can produce OLE objects. Choose the one you want and choose OK. Excel then starts the other application if it's not already running. You can then load a file or create something from scratch. When you're finished, exit the other application. You are returned to Excel, and the object you were working on in the other application is placed on the worksheet. To edit this object, double-click on it, and Excel restarts the application for you.

More stuff

Not all Windows applications support OLE.

Edit⇨Paste

Edit⇨Paste

Copies whatever is on the Windows Clipboard into your worksheet. This is the second step in copy/paste or cut/paste operations.

How you use it

After the cell or range is in the Clipboard (using the Edit⇨Copy or Edit⇨Cut commands), move the cell pointer to where you want to paste it and choose Edit⇨Paste.

If the cells in the paste area are not empty, Excel overwrites them without warning.

More stuff

If you used the Edit⇨Copy command to put the stuff in the Clipboard, you can paste multiple copies of the Clipboard contents throughout your worksheet.

Edit⇨Paste Special

Edit⇨Paste Link

Copies whatever is on the Windows Clipboard into your worksheet and creates a link to that data. Using this command is handy if you want a range to always show what's in another range.

How you use it

Copy a cell or range with the Edit⇨Copy command. Move to the location you want to paste it to and choose Edit⇨Paste Link.

Excel links the new range to the old range. If you change something in the old range, the changes show up in the new range.

You can also use this command to paste a link from data copied in another Windows application.

If the paste area is not empty, Excel overwrites the information that is already there without warning.

More stuff

If the source is more than one cell, this command creates an array. I can't explain arrays and the Windows Dynamic Data Exchange (DDE) here, but you don't have to know what's going on behind the scenes to use this command.

Edit⇨Paste, Edit⇨Paste Special

Edit⇨Paste Picture

Pastes the Windows Clipboard contents as a picture. The image also includes the row and column borders. **Note:** This command appears only if you hold down Shift while you choose the Edit command. You can use this command to bring in graphics from other applications.

Edit⇨Paste Picture Link

Edit⇨Paste Picture Link

Pastes the Windows Clipboard contents as a picture and creates a link to the original data. This command is useful if you need to show information from another application that may change.

Edit⇨Paste Special...

Lets you paste only part of a copied selection — or lets you paste a selection in special ways. Use this command when you want to copy only values (no formats), only formats (no values), or notes from a cell or range to another cell or range. It also lets you transpose a range — turn a vertical range into a horizontal range — when copying. Finally, it lets you perform a mathematical operation on data that was copied.

How you use it

Start by copying the cell or range. Then, move the cell pointer to a new position (or keep it where it is if you want to replace what you are copying). Choose Edit⇨Paste Special and choose the options you want.

This command is useful if you want to change a range of cells by a certain amount and don't want to bother with formulas. For example, to multiply all cells in a range by 1.05 (which effectively increases each of them by 5 percent), put **1.05** in a cell and copy it to the Clipboard with the Edit⇨Copy command. Then, select the range that you want to modify and choose the Edit⇨Paste Special command. Choose the Multiply option and choose OK. All the entries in the range are multiplied by 1.05.

More stuff

If the Clipboard contains data copied from another Windows application, Excel gives you the opportunity to do other things with the data when you choose Edit⇨Paste Special. For example, you can paste a link to a word processing document.

Edit⇨Paste

Edit⇨Redo [Action]

Reverses the effects of Edit⇨Undo. In other words, it undoes an undo. Use this command if you didn't really want to undo an action.

More stuff

This command appears only after you choose Edit⇨Undo, and it lists that actual undo operation that will be undone.

Edit⇨Undo

Edit⇨Repeat [Action]

Repeats the last thing you did. It's a great time-saver that can eliminate many trips to the menu when you're doing boring, repetitious things.

How you use it

Do something and then choose Edit⇨Repeat.

Most, but not all, actions are repeatable. The actual command name changes to tell you what will be repeated when you issue the command. Make sure you really want the command that's listed. If the action can't be repeated, the command reads, `Can't Repeat`.

Edit⇨Summary Info...

Displays some miscellaneous information about the current document.

This command does not appear unless the SUMMARY.XLA add-in file has been loaded.

The best use for this command is to store descriptive information about what a worksheet is for.

How you use it

Choose Edit⇨Summary Info and examine what it tells you. For example, it tells you how large the active area of the worksheet is. You can also fill in some of the blanks, such as a title, author's name, and description.

Formula⇨Note

Edit⇨Undo [Action]

Reverses the effect of the last thing you did. This command can be a real life-saver when you discover that the command you just issued didn't do what you thought it would do. You can also use this command to change something temporarily to see what happens (a sort of what-if). After checking out the results, use Edit⇨Undo to get things back the way they used to be.

How you use it

Immediately after you discover your boo-boo (and before you do anything else), choose Edit⇨Undo to restore your worksheet to its condition before the faux pas. The actual command name reflects what it will undo. For example, after you sort a range, the command reads `Undo Sort`.

It's vitally important that you don't do anything between the time that you make your mistake and the time that you choose Edit⇨Undo. You should get into the habit of looking at what you did before moving on to the next step.

Sometimes, what you are doing requires lots of memory and cannot be "undone." Excel always warns you in advance if you're performing an action that you won't be able to undo. In such a case, it's a good idea to save your worksheet first. That way you can undo the command by retrieving the saved version of your file.

More stuff

Ctrl+Z is a shortcut for Edit⇨Undo. Think of it as zapping your mistakes away.

Edit⇨Redo[u]Entry, File⇨Save

File Menu Commands

Care to take a guess what the commands in this menu deal with? Besides loading and saving files, you also find the commands used to deal with *printing*. This grouping is pretty strange, but Windows programs usually don't have a special menu called *Print*. Printing is almost always handled with commands in the File menu.

By the way, you can learn lots more about dealing with files in *Excel For Dummies.* You might want to start with the section entitled "Help, My Document's Gone and I Can't Find It" in Chapter 4.

File⇨Close

Closes a worksheet. If you haven't saved you worksheet, Excel politely ask you if you want to do so before it is removed from memory.

If you hold down Shift when you choose this command, it miraculously turns into Close All. This is a fast way to close down all the worksheets in memory in one fell swoop. (You still get a warning if a worksheet has not been saved.)

If you no longer need a file, you can free up some memory by closing it.

How you use it

Choose File⇨Close, and the active worksheet is shut down. It's that easy.

File⇨Exit

File⇨Delete...

Removes a file from a disk. If you need to free up some disk space, this command lets you do so without using other means (such as the Windows File Manager or DOS).

How you use it

Choose File⇨Delete; then choose the file you want to eliminate and choose OK. The files that appear are those in the current directory. Change the directory using the Directories list box or change the drive with the Drives list box.

Use this command with caution because a deleted file can't be recovered without resorting to some tricks of the trade — and even then, restoration is not guaranteed. Make sure you know what you're deleting. Erasing one wrong file can make your whole system inoperable.

More stuff

This command is mainly a convenience. There are lots of other ways to delete files from your disk — Excel just tries to make deleting files easy on you.

File⇨Close

File⇨Exit

Closes down Excel. If you have any unsaved work, Excel lets you know about it and gives you an opportunity to save it. Using this command is the proper way to exit Excel when you don't need to use it any more.

How you use it

Choose File⇨Exit and respond to any dialog boxes that Excel may present.

Don't get in the habit of simply turning off your computer when your work is done. A good practice is exiting all your applications first and then exiting Windows.

More stuff

Alt+F4 is a shortcut for this command, that also works in most other Windows programs.

File⇨Links...

Lets you update or change links to other worksheets or files. If your worksheet has references to other worksheets, this command forces them to be updated. For example, your worksheet might be linked to another worksheet on a network server. If the linked worksheet gets changed by someone, you can update the references with the File⇨Links command.

How you use it

Choose File⇨Links and then choose the appropriate option. If you want to change the worksheet that you're linking to, use the Change button and choose a new file. If you simply want to update the links, use the Update button.

More stuff

This command is not available if your worksheet doesn't contain any links.

File⇨New...

 Creates a new Excel file — either a worksheet, a chart, a macro sheet, or a workbook. Using this command is how you start a new project.

How you use it

Choose File⇨New and then choose the type of file you want to work on from the New dialog box.

 Contrary to its name, this command does not actually create a file on disk. Rather, it creates a *potential* file in memory. You must use the File⇨Save As command to actually save it as a file.

More stuff

The New dialog box may contain other listings besides Worksheet, Chart, Macro Sheet, and Workbook. These other things are templates that give you a head start in creating certain types of documents.

Shift+F11 is a shortcut for creating a new worksheet, Ctrl+F11 creates a new macro sheet, and the F11 key creates a chart sheet.

 This command is not the best way to create a chart. You are better off using the ChartWizard icon on the Standard toolbar, which walks you through the steps needed to create a near-perfect chart every time.

File⇨Open...

 Loads a file from disk into Excel so you can work on it. Using this command is how you work on something that's been saved to disk.

How you use it

Choose File⇨Open and then choose the file you want to load. The Open dialog box has a drop-down list box that lets you change the type of files that are displayed in the file list box. Normally, it displays only files with an XL* extension. You can change the type of files if, for example, you want to load in a Lotus 1-2-3 file. If the file is a text file, click on the Text button to get a list of text file options.

 You can choose more than one file in the Open dialog box. The trick is to hold down Ctrl while you click on file names. When all the files you want to open are highlighted, choose OK.

 Actually, Excel can read any file on your disk — but it can't always make sense of it. If your screen is filled with garbage after you load a file, it's a good sign that you loaded a file that Excel can't understand. A screenful of garbage is also symptomatic of trying to read an Excel file produced by a later version of Excel — for example, reading an Excel 4 file while using Excel 3.

More stuff

If you check the Read Only box in the Open dialog box, you cannot save the file with the same name (use the File⇨Save As command to give it a different name). Anticipating this mistake is a good way to make sure you don't accidentally mess up a perfectly good worksheet.

 If you tend to use the same worksheets all the time, you can save a few milliseconds of time each day by having Excel open them automatically. Simply move the worksheets to your \EXCEL\XLSTART directory, and they'll be loaded automatically every time Excel starts up.

Excel can also open files created by other programs. Use the list box labeled List Files of Type to choose a different file type to display.

Ctrl+F12 is a shortcut for this command.

When you choose the File menu, Excel displays the names of the last four files you've worked on at the bottom of the menus. If you need to open one of these files, selecting it from the menu is much faster than opening it using normal methods. Oddly enough, I've discovered that many people have never noticed this.

File⇨Page Setup...

Lets you specify some options that determine how your printed output looks.

Using this command lets you do any or all the following: change the orientation of the paper (landscape or portrait), change the paper size, change your margins, center the output on the page, print the spreadsheet row and column borders, remove the cell grids from printed output, ignore colors, specify a starting page number, scale the output, and change or remove headers and footers.

How you use it

Choose File⇨Page Setup and choose the desired options in the Page Setup dialog box. Don't overlook all those buttons along the right side — they lead to even more options. For example, the Printer Setup button lets you choose the printer to use (which is relevant only if you have more than one printer installed).

When you change settings with this command, they are in effect only for the current document — and are saved along with the document.

File⇨Print, File⇨Print Preview

Excel For Dummies explains all this stuff in more detail, beginning with the section entitled "In Pursuit of the Perfect Page" in Chapter 6.

File⇨Print...

Sends the current worksheet (or just the print range you specified) to the printer. Using this command is the only way to get your worksheet onto paper (short of photographing the screen).

How you use it

If you want to print the whole enchilada, just choose File⇨Print, make any adjustments in the Print dialog box, and choose OK. If you don't want to print the entire worksheet, select the range you want to print and choose the Options⇨Set Print Area command first. Then go for the File⇨Print command.

If you would like to print out the formulas in your worksheet, use the Options⇨Display command and choose on the Formulas check box. Excel displays the actual formulas rather than their results. Print the worksheet as usual and then go back and use the Options⇨Display command again and uncheck the Formula check box to get things back to normal.

More stuff

The Print dialog box holds quite a few options. Fortunately, they are all pretty much self-explanatory. If not to you, choose the Help button for an explanation.

If you find that your printouts are taking forever, try setting the Print Quality to a smaller number of dots per inch. This option reduces the quality of the output, but it may be good enough for draft printouts. Go back to 300 dpi for the final print job.

File⇨Print Preview, File⇨Page Setup

An entire chapter in *Excel For Dummies* (Chapter 6, to be exact) is devoted to printing.

File⇨Print Preview

Shows you, in the privacy of your own screen, exactly how your worksheet will look when it's printed. This display includes headers and footers.

Using this command can save you lots of time because viewing your output on screen is much faster than printing your work and *then* discovering that it was set up incorrectly. It also saves paper.

How you use it

Pretend you're going to actually print your work but choose File⇨Print Preview instead of File⇨Print. Excel displays the output in a full-screen window. The buttons at the top of the Preview window let you move to the next or previous page, zoom in or out, send it to the printer, go to the Setup dialog box, or quit the previewer.

More stuff

Notice that the mouse pointer is a magnifying glass in the preview
window. You can click on a specific part of the previewed output
to get a closer view. And you can use the scroll bars to move
around in a magnified view.

File⇨Print

File⇨*Print Report...*

Lets you choose a predefined report for printing.

This add-in is installed automatically when you install Excel and is
loaded when you choose the File⇨Print Report command.

Using this command is handy if you tend to make separate
printouts of various views of your worksheet that you've defined.
It eliminates the need to do all the setup work. Rather, you can do
all the setup once and give it a name. Then, the next time you
want to print the same thing, you just choose the name of the
report, and you're off to the races. This command works in
conjunction with the Window⇨View command and the
Formula⇨Scenario Manager command. Beginning users might
find this command rather confusing.

How you use it

The key to using this command is to use the Window⇨View
command first to create a view that includes the print area and
any other print options that you want. A report can consist of a
named view plus a named scenario (defined with the
Formula⇨Scenario Manager command).

Adding a new report in the Add Report dialog box can be kind of
tricky because you must click in the Current Sections list box
before you click on the Add button.

Window⇨View, Formula⇨Scenario Manager

File⇨*Record Macro*

Starts recording a new macro. This command does the same
thing as the Macro⇨Record command and appears only if you
don't have any documents open.

File⇨Save

Saves the current worksheet to disk. If what you're doing has any lasting value, using this command is how you can save it for posterity (or at least until you need to work on it again).

How you use it

Choose File⇨Save. If your document doesn't yet have an official name, Excel makes you give it one before it saves it.

More stuff

The default name for a worksheet document is SHEET*n*.XLS, where *n* is a number that starts with 1 and is incremented for every unnamed worksheet you open. You shouldn't save a file with this default name — and you probably wouldn't want to. The point of naming files is to make them somewhat meaningful to you and describe what they do.

Shift+F12 is a shortcut for this command.

You should save your file at a time interval that corresponds to the maximum amount of time you're willing to lose. For example, if you don't mind losing up to an hour's work, save your file every hour. Most people choose to save their work more frequently than this.

File⇨Save As

File⇨Save As...

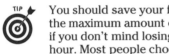

Saves the current worksheet to disk under a different name. Using this command is handy if you want to keep multiple versions of your work. You can save each successive version under a different name. That way, if you discover that you messed something up, you can always go back to an earlier version to recover from your error.

How you use it

Choose File⇨Save As and enter a new name in the File Name box. You don't have to give an extension since Excel supplies it for you.

If you enter a name that already exists, Excel lets you know about it.

More stuff

You can also use this command to make a backup copy of a file, simply by saving the file to a floppy disk (with the same name). After you do so, don't forget to save it again on your hard drive.

F12 is a shortcut for this command.

File⇨Save

File⇨Save Workbook...

Saves the current workbook to a disk file, with the extension XLW. Using this command is how you save your work that's stored in an Excel workbook.

How you use it

Choose File⇨Save Workbook.

More stuff

If you haven't set up a workbook, this command first groups all the open files into a workbook and then prompts you for a name.

If you need to give a bunch of Excel files to a colleague, you might find it more efficient to put all the documents into a bound worksheet. That way, you have only one file to be concerned with.

File⇨Save

If you don't know a workbook from a woodchuck, check out *Excel For Dummies,* beginning with the section entitled "Jot This Down in Your Workbook" in Chapter 9.

File⇨Unhide

Lists hidden files when you don't have any other documents open and unhides the file you choose. This command is the same as the Window⇨Unhide command.

Format Menu Commands

The commands under this menu pretty much all deal with changing the looks of things.

 As you might expect, *Excel For Dummies* addresses worksheet formatting. In fact, Chapter 3 is devoted entirely to this issue.

Format⇨Alignment...

 Changes the way information is aligned in cells. Using this command is how you change the way text and numbers are aligned within a cell. Besides the standard left-right-center alignment options, you can justify text, display it vertically, and even make words wrap within a cell (just like a word processor).

How you use it

Select the cell or range of cells that you want to align; then choose Format⇨Alignment. Choose the type of alignment you want and click on OK.

More stuff

You can set the alignment for cells even if there's nothing in them. Then, when you do put something in them, they will take on that alignment.

 The word wrap option is very useful for creating headings in tables because you can put long titles into a single cell, and Excel handles the word wrapping for you.

Format⇨AutoFormat...

 Applies one of 14 predefined table formats to a range of cells. Using this command is a very fast way to turn a dull table of words and numbers into an exciting, well-formatted table.

How you use it

Enter a table as you normally would, using values, formulas, and strings. Move the cell pointer anyplace in the table and choose Format⇨AutoFormat. Excel figures out the boundaries of the table and displays the AutoFormat dialog box with more than a dozen canned formats to choose from. Scroll through the list to get an idea of what the end result will be.

By default, this command changes the column widths — which may mess up stuff you have above or below the table. If you don't want all the formatting elements to be applied, choose the Options button and turn off any of the options you do not want. For example, if you don't want Excel to mess with the column widths, uncheck the Width/Height option.

Format⇨Font, Format⇨Border, Format⇨Patterns

Format⇨Border...

Lets you put borders around cells or a range of cells. The border can be either an entire box or just parts (like an underline). Using this command is one way to add some pizzazz to a worksheet. It also serves a more practical purpose by letting you set off various parts so they can be distinguished from each other.

How you use it

Start by selecting the cell or range that you want to add a border to; then choose Format⇨Border. Excel displays the Border dialog box, which lets you choose where you want the border, the style of the lines, and what color to make the lines. Choose OK to see the borders.

You might want to turn off the cell gridlines so the borders are more easily seen. Do this with the Options⇨Display command.

More stuff

Putting a border at the bottom of a cell is *not* the same as specifying underlining in the Font dialog box. Underlining affects only the characters in the cell, and if the characters spill over to adjoining cells, the underlining goes with it. A bottom border, on the other hand, is always exactly as wide as the cell. If you underline the contents of a cell that has a bottom border, the underline appears above the border.

Format⇨Bring to Front

Brings the selected object to the "top of the stack" when dealing with objects drawn on a worksheet. Using this command exposes a drawn object that's partially hidden by other objects.

How you use it

Select the object and then choose Format⇨Bring to Front.

More stuff

This command is available only when you have one or more objects selected.

Format⇨Send to Back

Format⇨Cell Protection...

Lets you hide the formulas in cells or lock cell contents and formatting so they can't be changed. Using this command is a way to keep others from changing the contents or formatting of cells or to keep others from looking at your formulas.

How you use it

Select the cell or range of cells that you want to protect; then choose Format⇨Cell Protection. Excel displays the Cell Protection dialog box. Choose Locked, Hidden, or both.

This command has no effect unless the worksheet is protected using the Options⇨Protect Document command.

Options⇨Protect Document, Format⇨Object Protection

Format⇨Column Width...

Changes the width of one or more columns. Some numbers are too wide to display in a cell, so you have to make the column wider to accommodate them. This command can also be used to hide columns or to adjust their widths so they are just wide enough to accommodate the longest entry.

How you use it

Select a cell or horizontal range of cells in the column or columns you want to adjust (you can also select entire columns). Choose the Format⇨Column Width command and choose the option you want.

The width of a column does not affect how much information it can hold. It affects only how much of the cell contents show up on-screen.

To unhide a column that has been hidden, you must first choose the column — which seems rather difficult to do because it is hidden. The trick is to use the F5 (Goto) key. After pressing F5, enter a cell address in the column that you want to unhide. For example, if column D is hidden, press F5 and enter an address such as D1 (anything in column D works). Then, choose Format⇨Column Width and check the Unhide button. Another way is to select a range of columns that includes the hidden column; then issue the command. The Unhide button unhides only the hidden column in the range.

More stuff

You might find it easier to change column widths by dragging the right border in the worksheet border (that has the column letters). If you select more than one column, all the column widths are changed.

You can quickly hide a column by pressing Ctrl+0 (that's zero, not oh). All the columns that have at least one selected cell in them will be hidden. To unhide these columns, select a range that includes the hidden columns and press Shift+Ctrl+0. You must use the 0 at the top of the keyboard, not the one on the numeric keypad.

Double-clicking on the border makes the column wide enough to display the widest entry in the column.

Format⇨Row Height

Format⇨Font...

Lets you change the font, style, size, or color of a cell or block of cells. It also works with chart text. Using this command is one way to make your worksheet more attractive and attention grabbing.

How you use it

Select the cell or range that you want to format; then choose Format⇨Font. The resulting dialog box has lots of options that will change the look of the selection.

Format⇨AutoFormat

Format⇨Group...

Combines several objects into one when working with objects drawn on a worksheet. If you're creating something that's made up of several different drawn objects, combining the objects into one object makes manipulating it (changing the size or moving it) easier.

How you use it

Select all the objects you want to include in the group and then choose Format⇨Group. To select multiple objects, hold down Shift while you select them or use the dashed rectangle tool on the Drawing toolbar to drag a rectangle around the objects you want to select.

Format⇨Ungroup

Format⇨Justify

Rearranges a single-column range of cells that contains text so the text fits into a specified number of columns. If you use large blocks of text in your worksheet to provide instructions or explanatory information, this command makes rewrapping the text to make it wider or narrower very easy. It's much easier than editing the cells individually.

How you use it

Select the single-column range of text; then increase the selection to include additional columns that represent how wide you want the text to be. Choose Format⇨Justify, and Excel redistributes the text to fit in the range you selected. To make text narrower, you must select additional rows to hold the text. If the text doesn't fit in the range you selected, Excel asks you if it's OK to go outside of the range. If you respond in the affirmative, anything that may be outside of the range is wiped out.

This command doesn't work with cells that contain values or formulas.

More stuff

You can use a blank cell to simulate a new paragraph.

Text box tool on the Standard toolbar

Format⇨Number...

Changes the way a number, date, or time is displayed. By default, Excel displays all numbers in General format — which usually doesn't look the way you want. This command gives you a great deal of control over how your numbers look, but it doesn't change the numbers themselves.

How you use it

Select the cell or range that holds values (or formulas) and choose Format⇨Number. Excel displays its Format Number dialog box. From the list box on the left, choose a format category; then choose a format code from the list on the right. As you scroll through the codes, Excel displays a sample so you can see what you're getting. When you find the right format, choose OK.

If none of the formats is quite what you had in mind, you can create your own custom numeric formats. Enter the formatting codes in the box labeled Code. Excel adds this format to the end of its list. Custom formats are valid only for the worksheet that you develop them in. Custom numeric formats can include text. For example, if you want some numbers to appear with a word next to them (such as Year 1, Year 2, and so on), create a custom format. In this case, you enter **"Year" #0** into the Code box.

With this format defined, you can enter a number such as **11** and format it with your custom format. It then appears in the cell as Year 11. And it's an actual number, not a label, so you can still use it in numeric formulas.

More stuff

You can use several shortcuts for common numeric formats:

Shortcut	Meaning
Ctrl+Shift+~	General format
Ctrl+Shift+!	0.00
Ctrl+Shift+@	h:mm
Ctrl+Shift+#	d-mmm-yy
Ctrl+Shift+$	$#,##0.00);($#,##.00)
Ctrl+Shift+%	0%
Ctrl+Shift+^	0.00E+00

Cell style list box on the Standard toolbar

Format⇨Object Properties...

Lets you specify how an object drawn on a worksheet is moved and sized relative to the cells that it sits on. It also lets you specify if you don't want the object to be printed.

This command is useful only if you use drawn objects (or insert graphs on a worksheet) and you're concerned about what happens to them if you change column widths. Actually, people usually use this command if they want to prevent an object from being printed. A good example is a text box with reminders to yourself. You might want to see this while you're working on the file, but you certainly don't want it to print.

How you use it

Select the object and then choose Format⇨Object Properties. Excel shows you a dialog box and lets you select what you want to happen to the object when the underlying cells are moved or resized. If you don't want to print the object, uncheck the Print Object check box.

Format⇨Object Protection...

Protects the selected object from being moved or changed. Using this command is a way to keep others from changing an object on a worksheet.

How you use it

Select the object or objects that you want to protect; then choose Format⇨Object Protection. Excel displays the Object Protection dialog box. Turn Locked on or off, as desired. If the selected object is a text box, you can also lock the text itself.

This command has no effect unless the worksheet is protected using the Options⇨Protect Document command.

Options⇨Protect Document, Format⇨Cell Protection

Format⇨Patterns...

Changes the background color and pattern of a cell or range of cells. When an object is selected, this command lets you adjust the weight of the lines.

Using this command is another way to add interest to your worksheet. A good way to make the parts easily identifiable is using different colors for different parts of your worksheet.

How you use it

Select the cell or range that you want to work with; then choose Format⇨Patterns. Adjust the Pattern, Foreground color, and Background color until the sample displays what you want. Choose OK.

If you make the background color the same as the foreground color, you won't be able to see the contents of the cell. Actually, you can put this command to use as a clumsy way to hide cells.

Format⇨Font

Format⇨Row Height...

Changes the height or one or more rows. You can also use it to hide rows. Making a row higher than normal is a good way to add vertical spacing between rows — sometimes better than using blank rows.

How you use it

Select at least one cell from the row or rows you want to adjust; then choose Format⇨Row Height. Enter the row size in points (72 points is equivalent to one inch). A height of zero hides the row(s). To reset row heights to default, choose Standard Height.

More stuff

You may find it easier to click and drag the bottom border of the row's heading.

You can quickly hide a row by pressing Ctrl+9. All the rows that have at least one selected cell in them will be hidden. To unhide these rows, select a range that includes the hidden rows and press Shift+Ctrl+9. You must use the 9 at the top of the keyboard, not on the numeric keypad.

Format⇨Column Width

Format⇨Send to Back

Moves the selected object to the "bottom of the stack" when dealing with objects drawn on a worksheet so that the selected object is completely or partially hidden by other objects. Using this command lets other objects, which may be partially hidden, be seen.

How you use it

Select the object; then choose Forma<u>t</u>⇨Send to Bac<u>k</u>.

More stuff

This command is available only when you have one or more objects selected.

Forma<u>t</u>⇨Send to Fr<u>o</u>nt

Format⇨Style...

Applies a predefined style to a cell or range of cells. It also lets you define and edit styles. Defining styles is a fast and easy way to apply consistent formats to cells and ranges.

How you use it

To create a style by example, format a cell how you want it; then choose Forma<u>t</u>⇨<u>S</u>tyle. Enter a name for the style in the dialog box and choose OK. Now you can apply all those formats to another cell or range by issuing the Forma<u>t</u>⇨<u>S</u>tyle command and then specifying your style name.

More stuff

If you choose the Define button, the dialog box expands and lets you change specific parts of the style or create a style from scratch.

A fast way to change the default font for everything on a worksheet is to change the definition for Normal style. Choose Forma<u>t</u>⇨<u>S</u>tyle, the <u>D</u>efine button, and then the <u>F</u>ont button. Change the font to what you want and choose OK. Everything on the worksheet that hasn't been assigned to a different style changes to the new font.

Format⇨Ungroup

Ungroups the object into its original parts when working with an object drawn on a worksheet that was grouped.

More stuff

This command is available only when a grouped object is selected.

Forma**t**⇨**G**roup

Formula Menu Commands

The commands on this menu deal with a variety of topics, including functions, range names, finding things, and outlining.

Formula⇨Apply Names...

Replaces ordinary cell references with range names that have been defined. Using this command can make your formulas easier to read. If you define a name for a cell or range, Excel does not automatically replace normal references in formulas with the names. This command forces Excel to substitute the names for the references.

How you use it

Select the range that you want to work on and choose Fo**r**mula⇨**A**pply Names. Excel presents a dialog box with several options. Usually, you can just accept the default options.

Fo**r**mula⇨**C**reate Names, Fo**r**mula⇨**D**efine Name

Formula⇨Change Name...

Lets you change the name you assigned to a cell or range.

This command does not appear unless the CHANGER.XLA add-in file has been loaded. If you decide that a name you gave to a cell or range isn't really appropriate, using this command is the best way to change it.

How you use it

Choose Formula⇨Change Name; then choose the name you want to change in the From box. Enter a new name in the To box and choose Close.

More stuff

You can also use this command to delete names you no longer need. Choose the Delete button in the dialog box to make these deletions.

Formula⇨Define Name, Formula⇨Create Names

Formula⇨Compare...

Compares the active worksheet with another worksheet and generates a report of everything that's different.

This command does not appear unless the COMPARE.XLA add-in file has been loaded. This command might be useful if you have two versions of a worksheet file and you want to know what, if anything, has changed.

How you use it

Make sure that both worksheets you want to compare are loaded, activate one of them, and choose Formula⇨Compare. In the dialog box, choose the worksheet that you want to compare it to. Excel creates a new worksheet with a report on it that tells you what is different between the two files.

Formula⇨Create Names...

Automatically makes names for cells or ranges, using labels stored next to the cells or ranges to be named. Using this command is a fast way to create several range names at once.

How you use it

Make sure that the range names you want to create are stored as labels adjacent to their respective ranges. Choose the names and the cells in the ranges to be named. Choose the Formula⇨Create Names command and tell Excel where the labels are relative to the cells. Choose OK.

If any of the range names already exist, Excel asks if you want to replace the old name. Be careful when responding because changing a definition for a range name could have drastic results on your formulas.

Formula⇨Define Name, Formula⇨Create Names

Formula⇨Define Name...

Lets you define a name for a cell or range or change a name that's been assigned. It also lets you change a range name or delete the name. Using this command is one way of setting up named ranges.

How you use it

Start by selecting the cell or range that you want to name. Choose the Formula⇨Define Name command and enter a valid name (it must start with a letter and have no spaces). Choose OK. To change an existing name or references, choose the command and then the name you want to modify. Either edit the name or edit the reference displayed in the Refers to box. Choose the Add button. If you change a name of an existing range, delete the old name with the Delete button.

Be careful when you delete range names. This operation can't be undone.

Formula⇨Apply Names, Formula⇨Create Names

Formula⇨Find...

Searches through the worksheet for a specific string or number. This is a fast way to locate something you're looking for without using the keyboard.

How you use it

First, select the range you want to search. If you don't select a range, Excel looks in the entire active worksheet. Choose Formula⇨Find and complete the dialog box that Excel displays. Choose OK to find the first occurrence. Then you can use the F7 key to find the next one (or use Shift+F7 to find the previous one).

Formula⇨Replace, Data⇨Find

Formula⇨Goal Seek...

Determines the value required in a cell that makes a specific formula return a value that you want. This command saves you the trouble of using trial and error to find a value that makes a formula return the answer you want. You might think of this as sort of a what-if in reverse. For example, if you have a worksheet set up to calculate the monthly payment for a loan, you can use Formula⇨Goal Seek to find the loan amount that results in a monthly payment that you can afford.

How you use it

Select the cell that has the formula for which you want to find a specific result and choose Formula⇨Goal Seek. Excel gives you a dialog box that asks for the value that you want the formula to produce and the cell that you want to vary. Click on OK to set Excel thinking. After it finds the answer, you can replace the old value with the new one by choosing OK or by choosing Cancel to keep the old value.

Sometimes, more than one value of an input cell produces the same result.

Formula⇨Solver

Formula⇨Goto...

Lets you specify a cell or named cell or range to select. Using this command is a fast way to select a named range or move to a specific place in your worksheet.

How you use it

Choose Formula⇨Goto and then choose the named range you want. You can also enter a cell or range reference directly.

More stuff

The F5 key is a shortcut for this command.

Formula⇨Note...

Lets you attach a note to a cell. You can use cell notes to remind you of what you were thinking when you created a formula or to provide instructions to others.

How you use it

Move the cell pointer to the cell that you want to attach a note to; then choose Formula⇨Note. Enter the note and choose OK. Excel reminds you that a cell has a note by displaying a small red dot in the upper right corner of the cell. You can double-click on a cell to read or edit its note.

More stuff

If you have a sound card and microphone attached to your computer, you can also record a voice note. But be careful; recording long voice notes can make the file size get very large.

Text box tool on the Utility toolbar

Formula⇨Outline...

Creates an outline from a worksheet that's set up appropriately. If your worksheet has hierarchical information — such as budget categories with subcategories — collapsing the categories to show only a desired level may be useful. This capability also works horizontally, so you can collapse months into quarterly subtotals, for example.

How you use it

Select the range that you want to outline and choose Formula⇨Outline. If you check Automatic Styles, Excel applies some built-in styles to the various outline levels. Choose the check boxes to tell Excel which direction you want the outline to go. Choose OK.

Not all spreadsheets are appropriate for outlines, and you usually have to do some upfront preparation to get the type of results you want.

Outlining tools on the Utility toolbar

Excel For Dummies gives you the lowdown on worksheet outlining. **Hint:** Open the book to the section entitled "We'll Have an Outline in the Old Town Tonight" in Chapter 5.

Formula⇨Paste Function...

Makes inserting a function into a formula easy. As an option, Excel also inserts dummy arguments for the function. Using this command is the easy way to insert a built-in function into a formula — especially when you're not sure of the spelling or the arguments.

How you use it

Start with an empty cell, or you can choose Formula⇨Paste Function while you're building a formula. Excel displays a list of all functions. Choose a category or leave All selected. Scroll through the function list until you find the one you want. If you check the Paste Arguments box, Excel also pastes dummy argument names along with the function. (You must replace the dummy argument names with actual references or names.) Choose OK.

When the Paste Function list is activated, you can jump quickly to a function by typing the first letter of the function.

More stuff

You can also press Shift+F3 to do the same thing.

You can check out Part V of this book for a listing of all Excel's built-in functions. Or, you can read Chapters 12 and 13 in *Excel For Dummies* for some real-live examples of functions that you might actually use at some point in your career.

Formula⇨Paste Name...

Makes inserting a reference to a named cell or range easy when creating or editing a formula. If you use named ranges or cells, using this command is a fast way to insert such a name into a formula. This command can also insert into your worksheet a reference list of all named cells and ranges.

How you use it

When you're building a formula and you need to insert a name, choose Formula⇨Paste Name and choose the name from the list. To get a list of all names, move to an empty area of your worksheet, choose Formula⇨Paste Name, and then choose the Paste List button.

If you use the Paste List button, Excel inserts a two-column list that overwrites anything that gets in its way.

Formula⇨Replace...

Replaces a specific text string or a number in a worksheet with another text string or number. Using this command is a quick way to make lots of changes. For example, if your company changes its name from NerdCom to GeekCorp, you can use this command to change every occurrence of the old name to the new name.

How you use it

Select the range you want to search. If you don't select a range, Excel looks in the entire active worksheet. Choose Formula⇨Replace and complete the dialog box Excel displays. Use the buttons on the right side of the dialog box to find additional matches or to replace everything.

Formula⇨Find

Formula⇨Scenario Manager...

Makes keeping track of various sets of input cells that you may want to change to calculate different scenarios easy.

This add-in is installed automatically when you install Excel and is loaded when you choose the Formula⇨Scenario Manager command. Spreadsheets are particularly adept at showing various outcomes (or scenarios) based on changing input values. This command lets you give meaningful names to sets of assumptions and then instantly change them. For example, your annual sales forecast might have *best_case, worst_case,* and *most_likely* scenarios. This command automates the process of plugging in a bunch of different values.

How you use it

Set up your spreadsheet with formulas and input values that affect the formulas. Select all the input values (changing cells) for a particular scenario and then choose Formula⇨Scenario Manager. You must provide a name for that particular scenario and then choose the Add button. Exit with OK. Then, you can insert different values for the changing cells and use

Formula⇨Scenario Manager to create a name for this scenario. Or, you can change the values in the dialog box (only if fewer than ten changing cells exist). To display the worksheet using a particular scenario, choose Formula⇨Scenario Manager, a scenario name, and OK.

More stuff

You can also create a summary report that shows how one or more formula cells change under each of the scenarios.

Formula⇨Select Special...

Automatically selects all worksheet cells of a certain type. Using this command is a fast way to locate and select cells that meet certain criteria. For example, you can quickly select all cells that contain formulas. People sometimes use this command as a way to check for spreadsheet errors. If you select all formula cells, you can often quickly spot a cell that should have a formula and doesn't.

How you use it

Select the range that you want to search in. If you don't select a range, Excel searches the entire worksheet. Choose the Formula⇨Select Special command and fill in the dialog box. Lots of options are here, so if you don't understand them, choose the Help button for more information.

Formula⇨Show Active Cell

Displays the part of the worksheet that contains the active cell. When you use the scroll bars to scroll around a worksheet that does not change the active cell, you can quickly get far removed from the active cell. This command quickly returns you to the place where the active cell is.

How you use it

Select Formula⇨Show Active Cell, and Excel scrolls the worksheet such that the active cell is visible.

More stuff

Using Ctrl+Backspace accomplishes the same thing.

Formula⇨Goto

Formula⇨Solver...

Lets you find one or more solutions to a problem that's set up properly in your worksheet.

 If this command doesn't appear, you need to rerun Excel's Setup program and tell it to install the Solver. This command lets advanced users who know what they're doing solve a variety of linear and nonlinear analysis problems.

How you use it

Sorry, but explaining this one is way beyond the scope of this book.

 Formula⇨Goal Seek

Formula⇨What-If...

Provides a way to store different what-if scenarios.

 This command does not appear unless the WHATIF.XLA add-in file has been loaded. I wouldn't recommend using this command. Using the Formula⇨What If command is a clumsy and confusing procedure; using the Formula⇨Scenario Manager is a *much* better approach.

 Formula⇨Scenario Manager

Formula⇨Worksheet Auditor...

Helps track down errors and potential problems in a worksheet.

 This command does not appear unless the AUDIT.XLA file has been loaded. This command can sometimes be useful if your worksheet isn't working the way you think it should or if you want to check it out for potential problems.

How you use it

Choose Formula⇨Worksheet Auditor, one of the four options provided, and OK.

More stuff

All the options except Interactive Trace generate a new worksheet with a report. The best way to see what types of information these reports contain is to try them out. The Interactive Trace option lets you find the cells that are used by a formula and also the formulas that a cell affects.

Help Menu Commands

These commands access a specific part of Excel's on-line help system.

If you need help to learn how to use Help, you really need help. If so, read *Excel For Dummies*, beginning in Chapter 1 with the section entitled "Help Is on the Way."

Help⇨About Microsoft Excel...

Displays a message that tells which version of Excel you're using, who the software is licensed to, How much memory is available, and whether your machine has a math coprocessor chip installed.

If someone asks you what version of Excel you're using or whether you have a math coprocessor installed, this command tells you in a flash.

Help⇨Contents

Displays the table of contents to Excel's on-line help system. If you're looking for general help, this command is a good place to start.

How you use it

After choosing Help⇨Contents, just click on a topic that looks as if it may helpful. And don't overlook the buttons in the Help window. You can use these to go backward and forward among the help topics and also to jump to the window that lets you search for a topic.

Help⇨Search

Help⇨Introducing Microsoft Excel

Starts up an interactive session that introduces new users to Excel. This command offers a pretty good overview to what's available in Excel. It comes up automatically the first time you run Excel after you install it.

How you use it

After choosing Help⇨Introducing Microsoft Excel, just follow the directions on the screen.

More stuff

If you have any documents open, Excel closes them before starting the introduction. If you haven't saved them, you'll have an opportunity to do so.

Help⇨Learning Microsoft Excel

Help⇨Learning Microsoft Excel

Starts up an interactive session that can help you learn about various aspects of Excel. Using this command is a good, and relatively easy, way to learn about a particular Excel topic. For example, if you finally decide that you want to determine what this toolbar business is all about, you can get a good explanation right on your screen.

How you use it

After choosing Help⇨Learning Microsoft Excel, just follow the directions on the screen.

More stuff

If you have any documents open, Excel closes them before starting the introduction. If you haven't saved them, you'll have an opportunity to do so.

Help⇨Introducing Microsoft Excel

Help⇨Lotus 1-2-3...

Provides special help for people who have used Lotus 1-2-3. If you know how to do something in 1-2-3 but can't figure out how to do it in Excel, this command sets you straight.

How you use it

Choose Help⇨Lotus 1-2-3 and then choose the 1-2-3 command that you know does what you want. Excel tells you how to do the same thing using Excel's menus — and even does it for you in some cases.

Help⇨Mutliplan...

Provides special help for people who have used Microsoft's old Multiplan spreadsheet (there must be one or two of them remaining). Beats me how it's used.

Help⇨Product Support

Tells about the types of support Microsoft offers and how to get help when there's nowhere else to turn.

If you're really stuck and the on-line help hasn't helped, the manual doesn't offer any solution, you can't find the office computer jock, and even *Excel For Dummies* doesn't come through, this command tells you how to contact Microsoft directly. You can contact them in several ways. If you choose the telephone route, be prepared to spend some time on hold because lots of other people are in the same boat.

Help⇨Search...

Lets you search the on-line help for a specific topic. Using this command is often the fastest way to get help on a specific topic or command. And, it may even be faster than using this book!

How you use it

After you choose the command, Excel runs the Help system and displays a dialog box. You can start typing a word or phrase, and the matching topic is displayed in the box below. Or, you can just scroll through the topic list until you find the one you want. Double-click on the topic, and you see a list of subtopics displayed below. Double-click on a subtopic, and you see information about it.

Help⇨Lotus 1-2-3...

Macro Menu Commands

Commands under this menu deal with macros — those sometimes confusing programs that can automate various things in Excel.

Excel For Dummies tells you just enough about macros to get by. Turn directly to Chapter 10 for more information.

Macro⇨Absolute Record

Changes the macro recording method to record absolute references. Recording absolute cell and range references is the default method. If you've changed the method to relative recording, this command gets you back into Absolute Recording mode.

Make sure that you really want to record in this mode. Usually, macros recorded with the Absolute Recording mode are less general than those recorded in Relative Recording mode.

Macro⇨Relative Record

Macro⇨Assign to Object...

Lets you assign a macro to an object drawn on a worksheet. Using this command lets you, or someone else, execute a macro by clicking on an object placed on the worksheet. This method is usually easier than using the Macro⇨Run command.

How you use it

First, put the object in the worksheet using a macro button, a graph, any geometric shape, or basically anything you draw on a worksheet using the icons in the Drawing toolbar. Select the

object by clicking it; then choose Macro⇨Assign to Object. Excel shows you a list of all the available macros. Choose one and then choose OK. From that point on, clicking on the object runs the macro.

Make sure that the macro always is available when the worksheet is loaded.

Macro⇨Run

Macro⇨Debug...

Helps you track down bugs in a macro.

This command does not appear unless you load the DEBUG.XLA add-in file.

If you create macros in Excel, using this command provides you with some handy tools to locate and correct logical errors you make.

How you use it

This command only executes if a macro sheet is the active document. Choosing Macro⇨Debug gives you a new menu system with only three menus. These menus contain all sorts of useful commands for macro freaks.

Macro⇨Record...

Starts recording a new macro. Using this command is how you record your actions to be played back later. In other words, you should create a macro if you don't want to type in all the macro functions manually.

How you use it

Choose the command, and Excel displays a dialog box that lets you assign a name to the macro, specify a shortcut key combination, and tell where you want to record it (either in the global macro sheet or in a separate macro sheet).

If you record a macro to the global macro sheet, Excel asks you if you want to save the changes when you exit Excel. If you choose No, the macro you recorded is not available the next time you run Excel.

More stuff

If you choose to record the macro in a regular macro sheet, Excel creates one if none is open.

Macro⇨Start Recorder

Macro⇨Relative Record

Changes the macro recording method to record relative references. When you choose this option, Excel records cell references relative to the current cell. It uses a different method to do this. Rather than record an absolute cell reference such as A4, it might record something like R[4]C[1]. This refers to the cell that is four rows above the current cell, and one column to the right. Usually, macros recorded in this way are more general than those recorded using the default absolute record method.

How you use it

You can choose this command either before you start recording or while you're recording.

Macro⇨Absolute Record

Macro⇨Resume

Starts macro playback again after it is paused. This command is used mainly when debugging a macro in Single-Step mode. This mode lets you pause macro playback, and Macro⇨Resume picks up exactly where you left off.

More stuff

This command appears only in the menu when macro playback has been paused.

Macro⇨Run...

Displays a list of available macros to run.

Using this command is one way to run a macro.

How you use it

Choose Macro⇨Run and then choose any of the available macros displayed in the dialog box.

Make sure that the macro you execute is appropriate. Macros are usually written for a very specific purpose, and you can't just go around running macros willy-nilly.

More stuff

Other ways to run a macro include pressing the key combination assigned to it and clicking an object (including a macro button) that has been assigned a macro.

Macro⇨Assign to Object

Macro⇨Set Recorder

Lets you specify the location in a macro sheet where a macro will be recorded to. This command is handy if you want to add on to an existing macro.

How you use it

This command is available only when a macro sheet is the active document. Move the cell pointer to the place where you want to start recording your macro; then choose Macro⇨Set Recorder.

If your selection is a single cell, make sure all the cells below it are empty.

More stuff

Every macro sheet has a range name called *recorder*. This command changes just the definition for that range name.

Macro⇨Start Recorder

Macro⇨Start Recorder

Starts macro recording at the cell in the macro sheet named *recorder*. This command doesn't create a new macro; rather, it lets you add on to or replace part of one that already exists.

How you use it

First, make sure you specify the location where macro recording starts, using the Macro⇨Set Recorder command. You must be in the macro sheet to do this.

Macro⇨Set Recorder, Macro⇨Record

Macro⇨Stop Recorder

Stops the macro recorder. Using this command is how you stop Excel from recording your actions.

Macro⇨Record, Macro⇨Start Recorder

Options Menu Commands

This menu may as well be called *Miscellaneous*. It has commands that do a bunch of different things.

Options⇨Add-ins...

Lets you specify which add-in files to load automatically whenever Excel starts up.

This add-in is installed automatically when you install Excel and is loaded automatically when you choose the Options⇨Add-ins command.

If you have some add-ins that you use a lot, using this command ensures that they are always available for your spreadsheeting pleasure.

How you use it

Choose Options⇨Add-ins, and Excel displays a list of add-ins that are loaded. If you want to add an add-in to the list, choose the Add button and locate the add-in file.

Loading add-ins takes memory away from your worksheets and can slow things down a bit. If you find that you don't really use an add-in that's always loaded, use the Remove button to remove it from the list.

More stuff

If the Options⇨Add-ins command is not available, use File⇨Open and load ADDINMGR.XLA from your EXCEL\LIBRARY directory.

Options⇨Analysis Tools...

 Opens the door to a slew of advanced analytical procedures.

If this command doesn't appear, you need to rerun Excel's Setup program and tell it to install the Analysis ToolPak.

This command runs any of several sophisticated procedures (most of them statistical in nature) that use the data in your worksheet. Your options are three types of analysis of variance (ANOVA), correlation, covariance, descriptive statistics, exponential smoothing, F-test, Fourier analysis, histograms, moving average, random number generation, rank and percentile, regression, sampling, three types of t-tests, and a z-test.

How you use it

After choosing Options⇨Analysis Tools, choose the procedure you want and follow the directions on the screen.

 The results of most of these procedures are in the form of a new range of data. These data are not linked to your original data, so if any of your input numbers change, you have to repeat the procedure to update the results.

Options⇨AutoSave...

Saves your worksheet automatically at a specified interval.

 If this command doesn't appear, you need to load the AUTOSAVE.XLA add-in file first. This command gives you one less thing to be concerned about.

How you use it

Choose Options⇨Autosave and then specify how often you want the file to be saved. You can also specify whether you want to be prompted first and whether you want all open documents to be autosaved.

Options⇨Calculation...

Controls how recalculations occur on the worksheets in memory. This command is used mainly to turn off automatic recalculation when you find that things slow down too much when you have lots of complex formulas.

How you use it

Choose the command and then choose the desired option in the dialog box.

 If you choose manual recalculation, the word CALC appears in the status line whenever the worksheet needs to be recalculated. You can't trust the values displayed until you press the F9 key to force a calculation.

Options⇨Color Palette...

Controls the colors used in the color palette for a document and also lets you copy a palette from one document to another.

Using this command is an easy way to make global changes to colors in a worksheet. For example, if you don't like the shade of red used, you can change it with the Options⇨Color Palette command. After doing so, everything that was previously red will change to the new color you selected.

How you use it

This command leads to a dialog box with the 16 colors displayed. To change a color, double-click on it and choose the new color from the Color Picker dialog box. To copy the custom colors from another document in memory, use the Copy Colors From list box and choose the document.

 It's pretty easy to mess up your color scheme completely. If you do so, you can return to the defaults by choosing the Defaults button in the Color Palette dialog box.

 Options⇨Custom Palettes

Options⇨Custom Palettes...

Lets you choose a color palette from a list provided by Microsoft.

This command is not available unless you load the PALETTES.XLA add-in file. Using this command is fast and easy, and the color choices are pretty good.

How you use it

Choose Options⇨Custom Palettes and choose a color scheme from the list presented.

More stuff

The list of color choices is based on a bunch of worksheets stored in your EXCEL\LIBRARY\COLOR directory. These options were put there when you installed Excel.

Options⇨Color Palette

Options⇨Display...

Controls various things about how the screen looks for the current worksheet only.

This command lets you customize your workspace by removing the gridline display, removing the row and column borders, changing the color of the gridlines, showing formulas instead of their results, hiding or showing automatic page breaks, and showing blanks in place of zero values in cells. Another handy use for this command is to turn off the display of drawn objects. You might want to turn off this display if you find that Excel is slowing down too much while it redraws objects and graphs.

How you use it

Choose the command and choose what you want to do.

More stuff

Be aware that this command operates on the current worksheet only. To make global changes in some aspects of screen appearance, use the Options⇨Workspace command.

Options⇨Workspace

Excel For Dummies explains more about your display options. Start with the section entitled "Putting on a Good Display" in Chapter 10.

Options⇨Group Edit...

Lets you specify which of the worksheets currently in memory you want to work on as a group. If you have several worksheets that all need the same formatting applied, you can do so in one fell swoop by editing them as a group.

How you use it

Make sure you have all the worksheets you'll be using loaded into memory. Choose Options⇨Group Edit, and Excel displays a dialog box that lists the loaded files. Choose or unchoose the filenames. When all are selected, choose OK. Excel displays the word [GROUP] in the title bar of all the worksheets in the group.

Getting out of Group Edit mode is very easy. In fact, you leave this mode when you activate a different document — even if it belongs to the group.

More stuff

You can't use the drawing tools while you're in Group Edit mode.

Edit⇨Fill Group

Options⇨Protect Document...

Lets you protect various parts of the worksheet so they can't be changed. You can also assign a password that's required in order to unprotect these things. Using this command is one way to keep others (or yourself) from messing up a worksheet.

How you use it

Choose Options⇨Protect Document and then choose the option you want. Before you issue this command, use the Format⇨Cell Protection command to specify cells to protect and the Format⇨Object Protection command to specify objects to protect.

If you specify a password, don't forget it. If you do forget the password, you'll never be able to make any changes to the worksheet.

Forma<u>t</u>⇨Cell Protec<u>t</u>ion, Forma<u>t</u>⇨Object Protec<u>t</u>ion

Options⇨Remove Page Break

Removes a page break that you inserted manually. If you no longer need a page to break, this command fixes the document so that it appears that you never entered that manual page break.

How you use it

Move the cell pointer to a manual page break and choose <u>O</u>ptions⇨Remove Page <u>B</u>reak.

 To quickly remove all the manual page breaks from a worksheet, select the entire sheet by clicking on the square where the row border meets the column border. Then, choose <u>O</u>ptions⇨Remove Page <u>B</u>reak.

More stuff

This command is available only when the cell pointer is next to a manually inserted page break.

<u>O</u>ptions⇨Set Page <u>B</u>reak

Options⇨Remove Print Titles

Removes print titles that you set with the <u>O</u>ptions⇨Set Print <u>T</u>itles command. Using this command is the easiest way to get rid of print titles that you no longer need.

How you use it

This command appears only when you select the entire worksheet by clicking the square where the row and column borders intersect. Choose <u>O</u>ptions⇨Remove Print <u>T</u>itles to cancel the print titles.

<u>O</u>ptions⇨Set Print <u>T</u>itles

Options⇨Set Page Break

Inserts a manual page break into your worksheet. This command lets you control where the page breaks occur when printing. For example, you might want a particular table within a worksheet to be printed on a page by itself. You can insert a manual page break in the row that the table starts in.

How you use it

Move the cell to cursor to the place where you want the page break to be; then choose Options⇨Set Page Break.

More stuff

Both manual page breaks and normal page breaks appear in the worksheet as dashed lines. You can distinguish the two types because the dashed lines for manual page breaks are closer together.

Options⇨Remove Page Break

Options⇨Set Print Area

Sets the print area to the current selection. If you don't want to print your entire worksheet, use this command to tell Excel what range you want to print.

How you use it

Start by selecting the range of cells you want to print. Then choose the Options⇨Set Print Area command.

More stuff

Excel automatically sets up a named range called *print_area* that corresponds to the area you set with this command.

After you set a print area, you can change it by modifying the range designation for *print_area*. Use the Formula⇨Define Name command to make this change.

Options⇨Set Print Titles

Lets you set up rows and/or columns that print on every page of your printed output. This command is particularly handy for very large tables that have column headings at the top and row headings along the left. If the table occupies more than one page when it's printed, this command makes it easy to see what's what on subsequent pages.

How you use it

Select the entire row(s) and/or column(s) that contain the title text and then choose Options⇨Set Print Titles. Excel displays them in a dialog box, and you can just choose OK.

Don't include the titles in the print area; otherwise, they will be printed twice on the first page.

Options⇨Remove Print Titles

Options⇨Spelling...

Starts Excel's spelling checker on the active worksheet. Use this command to avoid the embarrassment and potential public humiliation of turning in work with misspelled words.

How you use it

Select the range to be checked. If you don't do so, Excel checks the entire worksheet. Whenever it finds a word it doesn't recognize, Excel displays the word along with some guesses. You can double-click on a guess to replace it or use the buttons for other options.

Excel doesn't check the spelling of words in cells that contain a formula. However, you can force it to do so by editing the cell, highlighting the word or words to check, and then choosing the Options⇨Spelling command.

Just because your worksheet passes the spelling checker doesn't mean that everything's OK. Spelling checkers don't have any intelligence and won't warn you of a heading such as *United Snakes Production* when you meant to say *United States Production*.

Options⇨Toolbars...

Lets you choose what toolbars to display and also lets you create new toolbars and customize existing ones. You can save time by using icons on Excel's toolbars, but the correct toolbar has to be displayed first. Use this command to choose another toolbar to display.

How you use it

Choose Options⇨Toolbars, and Excel displays a dialog box with all the toolbars listed. Scroll through the list until you find the one you want and then choose Show. Or choose Customize to change the tools on a particular toolbar.

More stuff

You might find it easier to just right-click on any toolbar to get a list. Simply check a toolbar name to show it or uncheck it to hide it.

Part IV of this book explains more about toolbars. And Chapter 11 of *Excel For Dummies* reveals even more.

Options⇨Workspace...

Changes some of the global options for Excel that are in effect for all worksheets. Using this command is how you set the global defaults for Excel. More specifically, this command lets you set the number of decimal places displayed; specify R1C1 notation rather than A1 notation; show or hide the status bar, Info window, scroll bars, formula bar, or note indicator; and set several navigation options.

How you use it

Choose Options⇨Workspace and make your settings in the dialog box.

Options⇨Display

Window Menu Commands

These few commands deal with the way Excel's windows appear and operate.

Window⇨Arrange...

Arranges the windows of all active documents neatly on-screen. Using this command is a quick way to let you see all the open documents. You can then drag and resize them as you like.

How you use it

Choose Window⇨Arrange, and Excel displays a dialog box with four options: Tiled (arrange them like floor tiles), Horizontal (arrange them in a horizontal column), Vertical (arrange them in a vertical row), or None (does nothing but lets you adjust the windows synchronization without changing the window arrangement).

More stuff

Another option in the Arrange Windows dialog box lets you change the synchronization of the windows. This choice is relevant only when you're viewing multiple windows from the same document. When the windows are synchronized, scrolling in one window causes the other window(s) to scroll also. You can choose whether you want horizontal scrolling synchronization, vertical scrolling synchronization, or both.

This command is not available if all open windows are minimized (you'll see the Window⇨Arrange Icons command in its place).

 Window⇨New Window, Window⇨Arrange Icons

Window⇨Arrange Icons...

Makes the icons of all minimized windows arranged neatly at the bottom of the screen. Use this command if you're a neatness freak.

How you use it

Choose the command, and Excel lines up all the icons at the bottom of the screen.

More stuff

This command is available only if all open windows are minimized.

Window⇨Arrange Windows

Window⇨Freeze Panes

Freezes the row(s) above the active cell and the column(s) to the left of the active cell so they are always visible no matter where you are. This command can be handy if you want to be able to see row and/or column headers no matter where you are in your worksheet.

How you use it

Move the cell pointer to the cell at which you want the freezing to occur. Choose Window⇨Freeze Panes, and Excel freezes the column(s) and row(s) to the left and top of the cell pointer in place.

More stuff

If you haven't split your window with the Window⇨Split command, this command automatically creates new panes for you.

Window⇨Unfreeze Panes

Excel For Dummies tells you more about freezing panes, beginning with the section entitled "Immovable Titles on My Frozen Window Panes" in Chapter 5.

Window⇨Unfreeze Panes

Unfreezes frozen panes. This command is used to cancel the effect of the Window⇨Freeze Panes command and get things back to normal.

How you use it

Choose Window⇨Unfreeze Panes to thaw out your worksheet.

Window⇨Freeze Panes

Window⇨Hide

Hides the current document window. This command can get a window out of your way, yet keep it in memory ready to be used when necessary.

How you use it

Choose Window⇨Hide, and Excel hides the active document.

 Window⇨Unhide

Window⇨New Window

Creates a new "view" of the current document window. This command is handy if you would like to view two or more parts of a worksheet at once.

How you use it

Choose Window⇨New Window, and Excel opens another window with the same worksheet.

 Window⇨Split

Window⇨Remove Split

Unsplits a window that has been split with the Window⇨Split command.

More stuff

You may find it easier to drag the pane to the side of the screen to get rid of the split.

 Window⇨Split

Window⇨Split

Splits the current document into four panes, at the active cell.
When the current document window is split, this command turns
into Remove Split. Using this command is a way to view two or
four parts of a worksheet at once.

How you use it

Move the cell pointer to the place where you want the split to
occur and choose Window⇨Split.

More stuff

Dragging the small black bar at the top of the vertical scroll bar or
the left of the horizontal scroll bar to split the screen may be
easier than using the Window⇨Split command.

Window⇨Remove Split, Window⇨New Window

If you want to know more about splitting windows, see *Excel For
Dummies* beginning with the section entitled "Tapping on My
Window Panes" in Chapter 5.

Window⇨Unhide...

Lets you choose a hidden window to unhide. Using this command
is how you can reveal a window that has been hidden with the
Window⇨Hide command.

How you use it

Choose Window⇨Hide, and Excel hides the active document.

More stuff

A hidden window is still loaded into memory — you just can't
see it.

Window⇨Hide

Window⇨View...

Lets you create a named view of the current document — or lets you switch to a view that you've already named.

This add-in is installed automatically when you install Excel and is loaded when you choose the Window⇨View command.

Using this command is a real time-saver if you like to look at your worksheet in various ways at various times. "View," as used here, refers to the window size, position, frozen panes, cell selection, active cell, and settings in the Display dialog box (which you access via the Options⇨Display command).

How you use it

Set up a view of a worksheet that you like, choose Window⇨View, choose Add in the dialog box, and enter a name for the view. You can specify whether you want the view to include print settings and hidden rows and columns. You can create as many different views as you like and quickly switch among them with the Window⇨View command.

Options⇨Display

Window⇨Zoom...

Magnifies or reduces the contents of the current document. This command can give you a bird's eye view of your worksheet, so you can get an overview of how it's laid out and how objects and graphs are placed. Or, you can use this command to blow up your worksheet so you can read the text from across the room.

How you use it

Choose Window⇨Zoom and then pick a zoom factor between 10 and 400 percent.

This command does not affect the way a worksheet looks when it is printed. If you want to shrink or increase the size of your printed output, use the File⇨Page Setup command and adjust the Scaling parameter.

More stuff

You might also find the Fit Selection option useful. Start by selecting a range of cells, issue the Window⇨Zoom command, and then choose Fit Selection. This choice automatically sets the zoom factor so all the selected cells fit on the screen.

Zooming the worksheet down to a tiny size makes selecting large ranges easy. The best way is to move the cell pointer to one corner of the range to be selected; then hold down Shift as you click on the cell in the opposite corner.

Part III:
The Excel Chart
Command Reference

In this section you find an explanation of the commands available when a chart window is the active document. Some of the menus are the same or similar to those in a worksheet window. In the interest of eliminating repetitive, unnecessary, and superfluous redundancy, I simply refer you back to Part II, "The Excel Worksheet Command Reference."

If you're not familiar with how Excel deals with charts, do yourself a favor by checking out Chapter 7 of *Excel For Dummies*.

Chart Menu Commands

What would a chart window be without a chart menu? These
commands let you do a variety of things with your chart. Note
that some of the menus are identical to those available when
you're working in a normal worksheet window.

Chart⇨Add Arrow

Adds an arrow to a chart. Sometimes, you might want to add
some text and then use an arrow to point to a specific element of
the chart. For example, you might want to explain why a particular month's sales were so low. You can also remove the arrow
head to turn it into a normal line.

How you use it

After creating a chart, choose Chart⇨Add Arrow, and Excel sticks
an arrow into your chart. Then you need to move it and resize it
to make it look like what you want. To resize or reorient an arrow,
choose it and then click and drag on either of the black squares on
the end. To move an arrow, choose it and drag it to where you want
it to be. This command is usually used with Chart⇨Attach Text.

More stuff

You can change the line type, thickness, arrowhead style, and
color of an arrow by double-clicking on it. The Patterns dialog box
is displayed.

When an arrow is selected, the command changes to Delete
Arrow. You can also just press Delete to get rid of an arrow.

Chart⇨Attach Text

Chart⇨Add Legend

Adds a legend to your chart. If you have more than one data
series, a legend tells the viewer what the lines or bars stand for.

How you use it

After creating a chart, choose Chart⇨Add Legend and Excel
inserts a legend. You can drag it to another area, if you like.

92 Chart⇨Add Overlay...

If you included legend text in the chart series, the legend will make sense. Otherwise, it uses generic names such as *Series1* and *Series2*.

If you don't want to re-create the chart with ranges that include legend text, use the Chart⇨Edit Series command, select the series, and enter a name in the Name box. Repeat for each series. These names then appear in the legend.

More stuff

Double-clicking on a legend brings up the Patterns dialog box, which lets you change lots of things.

When an arrow is chosen, the command changes to Delete Legend. You can also just press Delete to get rid of a legend.

Chart⇨Add Overlay

Overlays a second chart over the main chart to create a combination chart.

You will have no need to use this command. It's much easier to use Gallery⇨Combination. This command is included for people who are accustomed to using it from earlier versions of Excel.

All Gallery commands

Chart⇨Attach Text...

Adds text to a chart. Using this command is how you add chart and axes titles.

How you use it

Choose Chart⇨Attach Text, and Excel displays a dialog box in which you specify what you want it attached to. It then inserts a text box with a descriptive word in it. You can edit this text in the formula bar just as you would with a cell in a worksheet.

If you want to add a free-floating text box that's not attached to anything, just start typing. Excel adds your text as a text box. Or, you can use the text tool for this addition.

Chart⇨Axes...

Lets you hide or display any of the axes in a chart. If, for some unknown reason, you need to get rid of one or more of the axes in a chart, you can do it here.

How you use it

After creating a chart, choose Chart⇨Axes, and Excel shows a dialog box with all the axes listed. To hide an axis, uncheck the appropriate check box and choose OK.

More stuff

This command isn't available when the chart is a pie chart (because they don't have axes).

Format⇨Scale

Chart⇨Calculate Now

Recalculates all worksheets and then redraws the charts. This chart is necessary only if you have recalculation set to manual.

How you use it

Choose Chart⇨Calculate Now.

If you have things set up for manual recalculation and the CALC indicator is displayed in the status bar, you can't trust that your charts are accurate until you issue this command.

More stuff

The F9 key does the same thing.

Chart⇨Color Palette...

Lets you customize the color palette and copy the color palette from one open document to another. This command is necessary only if you don't like the standard color choices.

How you use it

This command leads to a dialog box with the 16 colors displayed. To change a color, double-click on it and choose the new color from the Color Picker dialog box. To copy the custom colors from another document in memory, use the Copy Colors From list box and choose the document.

 It's pretty easy to mess up your color scheme completely. If you do so, you can return to the defaults by clicking on the Defaults button in the Color Palette dialog box.

 Format⇨Patterns

Chart⇨Edit Series...

Creates, deletes, or lets you edit a data series in the active chart window. This command is an easy way to add a new series to a chart, get rid of a series altogether, or change the worksheet range that the series uses.

How you use it

In a chart window, choose Chart⇨Edit Series. Excel displays a dialog box with all the data series listed, plus one called New Series. To change an existing series, click on it and edit the range(s) displayed to the right. To delete it, choose the Delete button. To add a new series, click on New Series and enter or point to a range.

 You can also copy a range from a worksheet with the Edit⇨Copy command and then use the Edit⇨Paste command in a chart window to copy the data. It is converted to a chart series.

Chart⇨Gridlines...

Displays or hides gridlines in a chart. Using this command is how you control which, if any, gridlines appear in a chart.

How you use it

In a chart window, choose Chart⇨Gridlines and then check or uncheck the appropriate choices.

More stuff

Some charts, such as pie charts, can't show gridlines. In these cases, this command won't be available.

Chart⇨Protect Document...

Protects or unprotects a chart's data series and/or window from being changed. You can also add password protection. Using this command is one way to keep others (or yourself) from messing up a good chart.

How you use it

Choose Chart⇨Protect Document and then choose the option you want.

If you specify a password, don't forget it; otherwise, you'll never be able to make any changes to your chart.

More stuff

When the document is protected, this command reads `Unprotect Document`. If it **is** protected with a password, you need to enter the password before it can be unprotected.

Options⇨Protect Document

Chart⇨Select Chart

Chooses the entire active chart. This command lets you apply formatting commands that deal with the chart itself — not the individual components.

How you use it

From a chart window, choose Chart⇨Select Chart. Now any formatting commands that you choose will affect the chart.

More stuff

You can also select the entire chart by clicking outside of the chart area.

Chart⇨Select Plot Area

Chart⇨Select Plot Area

Selects just the plot area of the active chart (the area within the axes). This command lets you apply formatting commands that affect only the interior of the chart.

How you use it

From a chart window, choose Chart⇨Select Plot Area. Now any formatting commands that you choose will affect the interior of the chart.

Chart⇨Select Chart

Chart⇨Spelling...

Starts Excel's spelling checker on the text in the active chart. If you use this command, your next presentation will look polished.

How you use it

In a chart window, choose Chart⇨Spelling. Whenever Excel finds a word it doesn't recognize, it displays it along with some guesses. You can double-click on a guess to replace it or use the buttons for other options.

Just because your chart passes the spelling checker doesn't mean that everything's OK. Spelling checkers have little or no intelligence and won't warn you of a chart title such as *Gross Income Four 1994* when you meant to say *Gross Income For 1994*.

Edit Menu Commands

The Edit menu commands in a Chart Window perform the same functions as in a Worksheet Window. See Part II.

File Menu Commands

The File menu commands in a Chart Window perform the same functions as in a Worksheet Window. See Part II.

Format Menu Commands

These commands let you control how various parts of your graph look. In most cases, you can just double-click on the part you're interested in, and you'll find your way to the appropriate dialog box.

Format⇨3-D View...

Controls the perspective and viewing angle of a 3-D chart. Sometimes, columns in the back of a 3-D chart can be hidden by columns in the front. This command lets you manipulate the view so you can see everything.

How you use it

When you have a 3-D chart displayed, choose Format⇨3-D View. You'll get a rather imposing looking dialog box that lets you manipulate the viewing angle and perspective by clicking on arrows or entering values directly. As you do so, a 3-D chart replica (not your actual chart) moves according to your com- mands. Choose the Apply button to make the changes to your actual chart (you may have to move the dialog box out of the way to see it). When you're happy with the new look, choose OK.

It's fairly easy to mess up a 3-D chart completely with this command. If that happens to you, click on the Default button to get back to the original view.

More stuff

You might find it easier (or at least more fun) to simply click on one of the corners of a wall of a 3-D chart and drag it around. If you hold down Ctrl while you do this, you can also see the bars (not just the wall move).

Format⇨Font...

Changes the font and/or type size used in a chart element. You can make the words stand out more by using larger type or a different font. Or, you can make axis text smaller so it's easier to read.

How you use it

Choose the chart object you want to modify (it must have text in it), and choose Format⇨Eont. The dialog box is just like the one you normally get when you change the font in a worksheet.

When you insert a chart into a worksheet, resizing the chart doesn't change the text size. Therefore, if you're going to put a chart into a worksheet, adjusting the text *after* you insert the chart is a good idea.

Format⇨Text

Format⇨Legend...

Lets you move the legend to another part of the chart window. If you have a mouse (and you should), you really have no need to use this command. It's much easier just to drag the legend with the mouse.

Format⇨Main Chart...

Lets you change lots of things about the chart. The main reason to use this command is that you can change chart types without losing any of the custom formatting you may have applied, which is what happens when you use the Gallery commands.

How you use it

In a chart window, choose Format⇨Main Chart and make your choices from the Format Chart dialog box.

Format⇨Move

Lets you move an object around in a chart window. The only time you would need to use this command is if you don't have a mouse attached to your system. Otherwise, it's much easier just to drag objects where you want them.

More stuff

Not all objects can be moved. If the Format⇨Move command is not available, the selected object cannot be moved.

Format⇨Overlay...

Lets you change lots of things about the overlay chart.

The main reason to use this command is that you can change overlay chart type without losing any of the custom formatting you may have applied, which is what happens when you use the Gallery commands.

How you use it

In a chart window, choose Format⇨Overlay and make your choices from the Format Chart dialog box.

More stuff

Obviously, this command won't be available if you haven't added an overlay to your chart with the Chart⇨Add Overlay command.

Format⇨Patterns...

Lets you adjust colors and patterns used for the selected object. You really have no reason to use this command. In almost every case, double-clicking on the object you want to format and then dealing with the dialog box that pops up is easier.

How you use it

Select an object, choose Format⇨Patterns, and make your changes.

Format⇨Scale...

Controls the scales displayed on the axes in the active chart. This command gives you lots of control over how your chart looks. It is most often used to change the upper and lower values on an axis from automatic to manual.

How you use it

Choose one of the axes on the chart and choose Format⇨Scale. You get a dialog box that lets you change several things about the axis. Notice the column of check boxes labeled *Auto*. If a box is checked, Excel determines that particular aspect of the axis. You can override Excel's choice by entering your own values in the text boxes. For example, you might want to compress the y-axis scale so smaller differences are more noticeable.

If you're making several charts that plot the same thing, you can easily mislead the viewer by changing the scales because people usually assume that the scales in similar charts are the same.

Format⇨Size

Lets you resize arrows and free-floating text. This command is useful only if you don't have a mouse. Mouse users can simply resize these elements by dragging.

Format⇨Text...

Lets you change the orientation and alignment of text objects in a chart window. This command gives you additional control over the way text appears in a chart.

How you use it

Choose the text object; then choose Format⇨Text. Make your selections in the dialog box and choose OK.

Format⇨Font

Gallery Menu Commands

Most of the commands in this menu change the active chart to another chart type. You may find that using the icons on the Chart toolbar are easier. Be aware that you can't necessarily show your data in any of these graph types. In other words, not all data are appropriate for all chart types. So use some discretion, OK?

If you change the chart type with a Gallery command after applying some custom formatting, you'll lose the formatting. Therefore, if you do any custom formatting, you might want to use the Format⇨Main Chart command to change chart types.

Gallery⇨3-D Area...

Changes the active chart to a 3-D area chart. A 3-D area chart can look pretty cool for some types of graphs — particularly line charts.

How you use it

In a chart window, choose Gallery⇨3-D Area; then choose from seven variations offered in the dialog box.

Format⇨3-D View

Gallery⇨3-D Bar...

Changes the active chart to a 3-D bar chart. This command can change the look of a chart drastically because it sends the bars out from the left, rather than traditional vertical columns.

How you use it

In a chart window, choose Gallery⇨3-D Bar; then choose from four variations offered in the dialog box.

Format⇨3-D View

Gallery⇨3-D Column...

Changes the active chart to a 3-D column chart. This command creates a common chart type that adds some dimension to your chart.

How you use it

In a chart window, choose Gallery⇨3-D Column; then choose from the seven variations offered in the dialog box.

Format⇨3-D View

Gallery⇨3-D Line...

Changes the active chart to a 3-D line chart. This command provides an interesting variation on normal line charts. The 3-D lines look like ribbons.

How you use it

In a chart window, choose Gallery⇨3-D Line; then choose from four variations offered in the dialog box.

Format⇨3-D View

Gallery⇨3-D Pie...

Changes the active chart to a 3-D pie chart. If you need a pie chart, this command provides a chart that looks much tastier than the normal 2-D pie.

How you use it

In a chart window, choose Gallery⇨3-D Pie; then choose from the seven variations offered in the dialog box.

Format⇨3-D View

Gallery⇨3-D Surface...

Changes the active chart to a 3-D surface chart. If you have lots of paired data points (as in an XY chart), using this command can be very effective. It's particularly fun to plot trigonometric functions because you can produce some very interesting surfaces.

How you use it

In a chart window, choose Gallery⇨3-D Area and then choose from the seven variations offered in the dialog box.

Format⇨3-D View

Gallery⇨Area...

Changes the active chart to an area chart. Using this command is sometimes a good alternative to using normal line charts.

How you use it

In a chart window, choose Gallery⇨Area and then choose from the five variations offered in the dialog box.

Gallery⇨Bar...

Changes the active chart to a bar chart. This command is useful if
you want your chart to be oriented horizontally rather than
vertically.

How you use it

In a chart window, choose Gallery⇨Bar; then choose from the ten
variations offered in the dialog box.

Gallery⇨Column...

Changes the active chart to a column chart. This command
provides a very common chart type.

How you use it

In a chart window, choose Gallery⇨Column; then choose from the
ten variations offered in the dialog box.

Gallery⇨Combination...

Changes the active chart to a combination chart. Combination
charts can show both columns and lines in the same chart. You
can also use two different y-axes, which can be useful if the scales
of the data series are drastically different.

How you use it

In a chart window, choose Gallery⇨Combination; then choose
from the six variations offered in the dialog box.

Gallery⇨Line...

Changes the active chart to a line chart. This command provides
a very common type of chart and is useful to show data that's on
a continuum. With this command, you can also create stock
market-type (hi-lo-close) graphs.

How you use it

In a chart window, choose Gallery⇨Line and then choose from
the nine variations offered in the dialog box.

Gallery⇨Pie...

Changes the active chart to a pie chart. This command is useful when you want to depict a data series in terms of relative proportions. You can plot only one data series with a pie chart.

How you use it

In a chart window, choose Gallery⇨Pie; then choose from the seven variations offered in the dialog box.

Gallery⇨Preferred

Formats the active chart with the settings you defined with the Gallery⇨Set Preferred command. Using this command is a fast way to create a bunch of charts with a similar look.

How you use it

Before using this command, you need to format a chart and then choose Gallery⇨Set Preferred to tell Excel that the chart has your preferred formatting. After you make these changes, you can create a new chart and then choose Gallery⇨Preferred to apply those formats to your new chart.

Gallery⇨Set Preferred

Gallery⇨Radar...

Changes the active chart to a radar chart. If, for some unknown reason, you would need such an obscure chart type, this command gives it to you.

Gallery⇨Set Preferred

Sets the preferred chart type to the current chart type. Using this command is a fast way to apply formatting to other graphs that you create.

How you use it

Start by creating a graph and applying all the custom formats you want. Then, choose Gallery⇨Set Preferred. This choice tells Excel to remember those formats. Now you can use Gallery⇨Preferred on subsequent charts to apply your formatting quickly.

Excel does not remember your preferred chart from one session to the next — unless you use the File⇨Save Workbook command to save your work in a workbook.

Gallery⇨Preferred

Gallery⇨XY (Scatter)...

Changes the active chart to an XY chart (also known as a scatter chart). This chart type is useful for many scientific applications.

How you use it

In a chart window, choose Gallery⇨XY (Scatter) and then choose from the five variations offered in the dialog box.

Help Menu

The Help menu commands in a Chart Window perform the same functions as in a Worksheet Window. See Part II.

Macro Menu Commands

The Macro menu commands in a Chart Window perform the same functions as in a Worksheet Window. See Part II.

Window Menu Commands

The Window menu commands in a Chart Window perform the same functions as in a Worksheet Window. See Part II.

Part IV:
The Dummies Guide to
Excel's Toolbars

A carpenter has a toolbox, and a spreadsheet junkie has a toolbar. Getting into the habit of using Excel's toolbars will save you lots of time and effort over the long haul. I've found that many people ignore these icons because they don't know what they do, and they're afraid that clicking the wrong one will screw something up. Actually, this fear is pretty much ungrounded, since you can use the Edit⇨Undo command to reverse the effects of almost anything that was done by a toolbar icon.

Chapter 11 of *Excel For Dummies* tells you even more about toolbars.

Excel's Toolbars

Excel 4.0 ships with nine ready-to-use toolbars (although one is pretty wimpy, with only one tool on it). You can also customize these toolbars by removing tools you don't need and adding other tools. And if you're really ambitious, you can create new toolbars that perform tasks that you do most often.

To display a toolbar, use the Options⇨Toolbars command and choose the toolbar you want. You can also click the right mouse button anywhere in a toolbar (except on an icon) to get a menu of toolbars. You can have more than one toolbar displayed, and you can move them wherever you like on-screen.

TIP You can click and hold the left mouse button on a toolbar icon to display a one-line description of the tool in the status bar at the bottom of the screen.

Customizing a toolbar is quite easy. First, make sure the toolbar you want to modify is displayed. Then, choose the Options⇨Toolbars command and click on the Customize button. The available tools are arranged by categories. Choose a category and then simply drag a tool to the toolbar that you're customizing. To get rid of a tool, just drag it off the toolbar. When you get the toolbar the way you want it, choose Close.

Now it's time to belly up to the toolbar and see what Excel is serving.

Chart Toolbar

The Chart toolbar, unlike the others, appears automatically whenever you activate a chart window or an embedded chart.

	Area Chart tool	Creates an embedded chart or changes the format of an active or selected embedded chart to a 2-D area chart.
	Bar Chart tool	Creates an embedded chart or changes the active or selected embedded chart to a 2-D bar chart.
	Column Chart tool	Creates an embedded chart or changes the active or selected embedded chart to a 2-D column chart.
	Stacked Column Chart tool	Creates an embedded chart or changes the active or selected embedded chart to a 2-D stacked column chart.

	Line Chart tool	Creates an embedded chart or changes the active or selected embedded chart to a normal 2-D line chart.
	Pie Chart tool	Creates an embedded chart or changes the active or selected embedded chart to a 2-D pie chart with the value labels shown as percentages.
	XY (Scatter) Chart tool	Creates an embedded chart or changes the active or selected embedded chart to an XY (scatter) chart with data point makers.
	3-D Area Chart tool	Creates an embedded chart or changes the active or selected embedded chart to a 3-D area chart.
	3-D Bar Chart tool	Creates an embedded chart or changes the active or selected embedded chart to a 3-D bar chart.
	3-D Column Chart tool	Creates an embedded chart or changes the active or selected embedded chart to a 3-D column chart.
	3-D Perspective Column Chart tool	Creates an embedded chart or changes the active or selected embedded chart to a 3-D column chart with each series plotted separately.
	3-D Line Chart tool	Creates an embedded chart or changes the active or selected embedded chart to a 3-D line chart (the lines look like ribbons).
	3-D Pie Chart tool	Creates an embedded chart or changes the active or selected embedded chart to a 3-D pie chart with the value labels shown as percentages.
	3-D Surface Chart tool	Creates an embedded chart or changes the active or selected embedded chart to a 3-D surface chart.
	Radar Chart tool	Creates an embedded chart or changes the active or selected embedded chart to a radar chart with lines and markers.

	Line/Column Chart tool	Creates an embedded chart or changes the active or selected embedded chart to a combination chart (lines and columns).
	Volume/Hi-Lo-Close	Creates an embedded chart or changes the active or selected embedded chart to a stock market-type chart.
	Preferred Chart tool	Creates an embedded chart on a worksheet using the selected cells in the area you specify by dragging the mouse and, in the format you set, using the <u>G</u>allery⇨Se<u>t</u> Preferred command.
	ChartWizard tool	Starts the ChartWizard so you can create a chart as an embedded object on a worksheet or edit an embedded chart or chart in its own window.
	Horizontal Gridlines tool	Adds or removes major value axis gridlines visible on an active chart or selected embedded chart.
	Legend tool	Adds or removes a legend along the right side of an active chart or selected embedded chart.
	Arrow tool	Creates an arrow on the active chart (it also works on worksheets and macro sheets).
	Text Box tool	Lets you add unattached text to a the active chart and also draws a text box on a worksheet.

Drawing Toolbar

This toolbar is useful if you want to add drawings or create objects on your worksheet.

	Line tool	Draws a straight line.
	Arrow tool	Creates an arrow on a worksheet or macro sheet or puts an arrow on the active chart.
	Freehand tool	Lets you draw freehand lines.

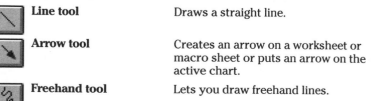

Text Box tool
Draws a text box on a worksheet or lets you add unattached text to a chart.

 Button tool
Draws a button to which you can assign a macro. When you click the button, the macro executes.

Selection tool
Selects one or more graphic objects.

 Reshape tool
Lets you change the shape of a polygon.

Rectangle tool
Draws a rectangle or a square.

Oval tool
Draws an oval or a circle.

Arc tool
Draws an arc or a circle segment.

Polygon tool
Draws a polygon.

Freehand Polygon tool
Draws a shape that is a combination of freehand and straight lines.

 Filled Rectangle tool
Draws a rectangle or square that's filled with the window background pattern and color.

 Filled Oval tool
Draws an oval or circle that's filled with the window background pattern and color.

 Filled Arc tool
Draws a circle segment that's one-quarter of a full circle and filled with the window background pattern and color.

 Filled Polygon tool
Draws a polygon that's filled with the window background pattern and color.

Filled Freehand Polygon tool
Draws a freehand polygon shape that's filled with the window background pattern and color.

 Group tool
Combines a group of graphic objects into a single object.

Ungroup tool
Separates grouped objects into individual objects.

Bring to Front tool
Places one or more selected objects in front of all other objects.

	Send to Back tool	Places one or more selected objects behind all other objects.
	Color tool	Changes the foreground color of a selected cell or object.
	Dark Shading tool	Applies a dark shading pattern to selected cells and graphic objects.
	Light Shading tool	Applies a light shading pattern to selected cells and graphic objects.
	Drop Shadow tool	Adds a shadow to the bottom and the right side of a selected cell or range.

Formatting Toolbar

This toolbar has lots of useful formatting tools on it.

	Outline Border tool	Adds or removes a border around the outermost edges of the selected cells.
	Left Border tool	Adds or removes a border along the left edge of each selected cell.
	Right Border tool	Adds or removes a border along the right edge of each selected cell.
	Top Border tool	Adds or removes a border along the upper edge of each selected cell.
	Bottom Border tool	Adds or removes a border along the lower edge of each selected cell.
	Bottom Double Border tool	Adds or removes a double border along the lower edge of each of the selected cells.
	Dark Shading tool	Applies a dark shading pattern to selected cells and graphic objects.
	Light Shading tool	Applies a light shading pattern to selected cells and graphic objects.
	AutoFormat tool	Automatically formats a range of cells by recognizing header rows and columns, summary rows and columns, and other elements of a table.
	Currency Style tool	Applies the currency style to selected cells.
	Percent Style tool	Applies the percent style to selected cells.

	Comma Style tool	Applies the comma style to selected cells.
	Increase Decimal tool	Displays an additional decimal place to the selected numeric cells each time you click it.
	Decrease Decimal tool	Removes one decimal place from the displayed numeric cells each time you click it.
Normal	**Style box**	Applies a cell style to the selection or lets you define a style based on the current selection.

Formula Toolbar

Personally, I don't find this toolbar too useful. Most of these tools merely spit out a single character that is frequently used in formulas. It's much quicker just to type the character.

	Equal Sign tool	Adds an equal sign (=) at the location of the insertion point in the formula bar.
	Plus Sign tool	Adds a plus sign (+) at the location of the insertion point in the formula bar.
	Minus Sign tool	Adds a minus sign (-) at the location of the insertion point in the formula bar.
	Multiplication Sign tool	Adds an asterisk (*) at the location of the insertion point in the formula bar.
	Division Sign tool	Adds a division sign (/) at the location of the insertion point in the formula bar.
	Exponentiation Sign tool	Adds a caret (^) at the location of the insertion point in the formula bar.
	Left Parenthesis tool	Adds an opening parenthesis [( ] at the location of the insertion point in the formula bar.
	Right Parenthesis tool	Adds a closing parenthesis [ )] at the location of the insertion point in the formula bar.
	Colon tool	Adds a colon (:) at the location of the insertion point in the formula bar.

	Comma tool	Adds a comma (,) at the location of the insertion point in the formula bar.
	Percent Sign tool	Adds a percent sign (%) at the location of the insertion point in the formula bar.
	Dollar Sign tool	Adds a dollar sign ($) at the location of the insertion point in the formula bar.
	AutoSum tool	Inserts into the active cell a formula with the =SUM function and a proposed sum range. The proposed range is based on the data above or to the left of the active cell.
	Paste Function tool	Displays the Paste Function dialog box so that you can insert a selected function into the formula bar.
	Paste Names tool	Displays the Paste Names dialog box so that you can insert a selected name into the formula bar.
	Constrain Numeric tool	Constrains handwriting recognition to numbers and punctuation only — relevant only if you have a computer with pen input.

Macro Toolbar

This toolbar is useful for macro freaks.

	Record Macro tool	Records your actions and commands to create a macro.
	Stop Recording Macro tool	Stops recording a macro.
	Run Macro tool	Runs the currently selected macro, starting at the active cell.
	Step Macro tool	Displays the Single Step dialog box so you can step through the current macro one cell at a time, starting at the active cell.
	Resume Macro tool	Resumes a macro operation after the macro has been paused.
	Paste Function tool	Displays the Paste Function dialog box so that you can insert a selected function into the formula bar.

Paste Names tool

Displays the Paste Names dialog box so that you can insert a selected name into the formula bar.

Macro Paused Toolbar

This toolbar has a grand total of one tool on it. This toolbar displays automatically when a macro is paused.

 Macro Resume tool

Resumes a macro operation after the macro has been paused.

Microsoft Excel 3.0 Toolbar

This toolbar was included for those people who got used to the single toolbar available in Excel 3.0.

| Normal | **Style Box** | Applies a cell style to the selection or lets you define a style based on the current selection. |

 Promote tool

Raises selected rows or columns one level higher in an outline.

 Demote tool

Moves selected rows or columns one level lower in an outline.

 Show Outline Symbols tool

Creates an outline, if one doesn't exist, and displays or hides the outline symbols on your worksheet.

 Select Visible Cells tool

Selects the visible cells on a worksheet so changes you make affect only the visible cells (not the hidden rows or columns).

 AutoSum tool

Inserts into the active cell a formula with the =SUM function and a proposed sum range. The proposed range is based on the data above or to the left of the active cell.

 Bold tool

Applies bold formatting to selected text in text boxes and buttons or to the text in a selected cell.

 Italic tool

Applies italic formatting to selected text in text boxes and buttons or to the text in a selected cell.

Left Align tool

Aligns the contents of a selected text box, button, or cell to the left.

 Center Align tool

Centers the contents of a selected text box, button, or cell.

Right Align tool

Aligns the contents of a selected text box, button, or cell to the right.

 Selection tool

Selects one or more graphic objects.

 Line tool

Draws a straight line.

 Filled Rectangle tool

Draws a rectangle or square that's filled with the window background pattern and color.

 Filled Oval tool

Draws an oval or circle that's filled with the window background pattern and color.

Arc tool

Draws an arc or a circle segment.

 Preferred Chart tool

Creates an embedded chart on a worksheet using the selected cells in the area you specify by dragging the mouse and in the format you set using the Gallery⇨Set Preferred command.

 Text Box tool

Lets you add unattached text to the active chart and also draws a text box on a worksheet.

Button tool

Draws a button to which you can assign a macro. When you click on the button, the macro runs.

Camera tool

Creates a picture of a selected range of cells on a chart and pastes the picture as an object on a worksheet or chart. The picture is linked to the source selection.

Standard Toolbar

This is the toolbar that is displayed by default.

 New Worksheet tool

Creates a new worksheet.

	Open File tool	Displays the Open dialog box so you can load a document from disk.
	Save File tool	Saves changes made to the active document.
	Print tool	Prints the active document according to the options you specified in the Print dialog box.
	Style Box	Applies a cell style to the selection or lets you define a style based on the current selection.
	AutoSum tool	Inserts into the active cell a formula with the =SUM function and a proposed sum range. The proposed range is based on the data above or to the left of the active cell.
	Bold tool	Applies bold formatting to selected text in text boxes and buttons or to the text in a selected cell.
	Italic tool	Applies italic formatting to selected text in text boxes and buttons or to the text in a selected cell.
	Increase Font Size tool	Increases the font size of the selected text to the next larger size in the Font Size list box each time you click on it.
	Decrease Font Size tool	Decreases the font size of the selected text to the next smaller size in the Font Size list box each time you click on it.
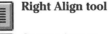	**Left Align tool**	Aligns the contents of a selected text box, button, or cell to the left.
	Center Align tool	Centers the contents of a selected text box, button, or cell.
	Right Align tool	Aligns the contents of a selected text box, button, or cell to the right.
	Center Across Columns tool	Centers the text from one cell horizontally across selected columns.
	AutoFormat tool	Automatically formats a range of cells by recognizing header rows and columns, summary rows and columns, and other elements of a table.
	Outline Border tool	Adds a border around the outermost edges of the selected cells.

Bottom Border tool — Adds a bottom border to the selected cell.

 Copy tool — Copies the selected cells, characters, or objects onto the Clipboard.

 Paste Formats tool — Pastes into the selection only the cell formats from the cells that you have copied onto the Clipboard.

ChartWizard tool — Starts the ChartWizard so that you can edit an embedded chart or chart document or create a new chart as an embedded object on a worksheet.

Help tool — Adds a question mark (?) to the mouse pointer. When you place the new pointer over a command name or screen region and click on the mouse button, you get information about that command or screen region.

Utility Toolbar

This toolbar has a bunch of miscellaneous tools.

 Undo tool — Reverses the effect of most commands or deletes the last entry you typed.

Repeat tool — Repeats the last command you chose, if possible, including any dialog box option settings.

 Copy tool — Copies the selected cells, characters, or objects onto the Clipboard.

 Paste Values tool — Pastes into the current selection only the values from the cells that you have copied to the Clipboard.

 Paste Formats tool — Pastes into the current selection only the cell formats from the cells that you have copied to the Clipboard.

 Zoom In tool — Allows you to see more detail by changing the scale of the document to the next higher magnification.

 Zoom Out tool — Allows you to see more of the document by changing the scale to the next lower magnification.

Sort Ascending tool Rearranges the rows of a selection in sorted ascending order.

 Sort Descending tool Rearranges the rows of a selection in sorted descending order.

 Lock Cell tool Prevents selected cells and objects from being changed when the document is protected.

 Promote tool Raises selected rows or columns one level higher in an outline.

 Demote tool Moves selected rows or columns one level lower in an outline.

 Show Outline Symbols tool Creates an outline, if one does not exist, and displays or hides the outline symbols on your worksheet.

 Select Visible Cells tool Selects the visible cells within the current selection that crosses hidden rows or columns so that changes you make affect only the visible cells and not the hidden rows or columns.

 Button tool Draws a button to which you can assign a macro. When you click the button, the macro executes.

 Text Box tool Lets you add unattached text to a the active chart and also draws a text box on a worksheet.

Camera tool Creates a picture of a selected range of cells as an object on a worksheet. The picture is linked to the source selection.

Check Spelling tool Checks the spelling of the text in worksheets, macro sheets, charts, graphic objects, or the formula bar.

Set Print Area tool Defines the area of the active worksheet that you want to print.

Calculate Now tool Calculates all open worksheets, macro sheets, and charts or a formula in the active formula bar.

Part V:
The Dummies Guide to Excel's Worksheet Functions

Excel provides a boatload of built-in worksheet functions — far too many for people who write books about Excel. You can use these functions to do special calculations. Besides worksheet functions, Excel also has a ton of macro functions, which are described in Part VI.

For more background on Excel's functions, check out Chapters 12 and 13 in *Excel For Dummies*.

Excel's Worksheet Functions

Most worksheet functions take arguments, which are always enclosed in parentheses and separated by commas (with no spaces in between). Even if a function doesn't need an argument, you must insert a pair of empty parentheses. The arguments can be references to cells, actual numbers, or strings. When Excel "evaluates" a function, it returns a single value or label.

Don't be afraid to consult the on-line help for even more information about a specific function. Here's how. Press the F1 key or choose Help. Then, from the Help window, choose Worksheet Functions, the category, and finally, the specific function you need help with.

The following pages summarize what each of these worksheet functions can do for you. They are listed in alphabetical order.

Note: Excel's analysis toolpak add-in includes many more advanced functions, which are used primarily for special purposes. These functions are not covered in here.

ABS(number)

Absolute value. Returns the absolute (positive) value of *number*. ABS of a positive number is the number, of 0 equals 0, and of a negative number is the number multiplied by –1 (similar to truncating the minus sign). The absolute value of a label returns the #VALUE! error. Use ABS when you need a number as a positive value.

ACOS(number)

Arccosine. Returns the arccosine of *number* in radians. *Number* must be from –1 to 1. ACOS returns the angle of a cosine if *number* is a cosine value. ACOS is the reciprocal of COS.

ACOSH(number)

Hyperbolic arccosine. Returns the inverse hyperbolic cosine of *number*. *Number* must be greater than or equal to 1. ACOSH is the reciprocal of COSH.

ADDRESS(row_num,column_num, abs_num,a1,sheet_text)

Cell address. Returns a cell address as text based on the row number (*row_num*) and the column letter (*col_num*) of the cell. The three optional arguments have the following syntax:

Argument	Description	Option	Result
abs_num	Cell address type	1	Absolute reference (A1)
		2	Absolute row, relative column (A$1)
		3	Relative row, absolute column ($A1)
		4	Relative reference (A1)
a1	Reference style	TRUE or omitted	A1
		FALSE	R1C1
sheet_text	Spreadsheet or macro sheet name		

AND(logical1,logical2,...)

And. Returns TRUE if all arguments are TRUE; returns FALSE if one or more arguments are FALSE. A maximum of 30 arguments can exist.

AREAS(reference)

Number of areas. Returns the number of areas in *reference,* a single or contiguous range of cells.

ASIN(number)

Arcsine. Returns the arcsine of *number* in radians. *Number* must be from −1 to 1. Returns the angle of a sine if *number* is a sine value. ASIN is the reciprocal of SIN.

ASINH(number)

Hyperbolic arcsine. Returns the inverse hyperbolic sine of *number. Number* must be from −1 to 1. Returns the angle of a sine if *number* is a sine value. ASINH is the reciprocal of SINH.

ATAN(number)

Arctangent. Returns the arctangent of *number* as a radian angle, −p/2 to p/2 (−90 to 90 degrees). Returns the angle of a tangent if *number* is a tangent value. ATAN is the reciprocal of TAN.

ATAN2(*x_number*,*y_number*)

Four-quadrant arctangent. Returns the arctangent of the coordinate values of *x_number* and *y_number* as a radian angle, –p2 to p2 (–180 to 180 degrees), excluding p. *X_number* and *y_number* must be greater than 1 or #DIV/0! is returned.

ATANH(*number*)

Hyperbolic arctangent. Returns the inverse hyperbolic tangent of *number*. ATANH is the reciprocal of TANH.

AVERAGE(*number1*,*number2*,...)

Average. Calculates the average, or arithmetic mean, of *numbers*. A maximum of 30 arguments containing values can exist. AVERAGE ignores blank cells but includes zero values.

CELL(*info_type*,*reference*)

Cell content information. Returns the specified attribute information about the *reference* cell, or active cell. *Info_type* can be one of the following:

Attribute	Returns
"address"	Cell address of the first cell in *reference* in text form.
"col"	Column number of the cell in *reference*.
"color"	1 if the cell is formatted for color for negative values; otherwise, 0.
"contents"	Cell contents of the upper left cell in *reference*.
"filename"	Path and filename that contain *reference* in text form. Unsaved files return ("").
"format"	Number format of *reference* in text form. Include – at the end if formatted for color for negative values and () at the end if formatted for parentheses.
"parentheses"	1 if *reference* is formatted for parentheses; otherwise, 0.
"prefix"	Label prefix for text alignment in text form.
"protect"	0 if *reference* is not locked; 1 if *reference* is locked.
"row"	Row number of the cell in *reference*.
"type"	Text value for the type of cell content of *reference*.
"width"	Column width of the cell in *reference*, rounded to the nearest integer.

CHAR(number)

Character for the code. Returns the character equivalent to the ASCII code *number*. *Number* is 1 through 255.

CHOOSE(index_num,value1,value2,...)

Choose a value or text. Returns a value from the list of arguments as specified by *index_num*. A maximum of 29 arguments can exist.

CLEAN(text)

Clean nonprinting text. Returns *text* without nonprinting characters, ASCII 1 – 32 and 127 – 255.

CODE(text)

Code for the character. Returns the ASCII code number equivalent for the first letter of *text*.

COLUMN(reference)

Column number. Returns the column number of the cell *reference*, where column A = 1, B = 2, and so on. A multiple cell *reference* returns a horizontal array of column numbers. If *reference* is omitted, returns the column number of COLUMN's cell address.

COLUMNS(array)

Number of columns. Returns the number of columns in *array*.

COS(number)

Cosine. Returns the cosine of *number* as a radian angle. COS is the reciprocal of ACOS.

COSH(number)

Hyperbolic cosine. Returns the hyperbolic cosine of *number*. COSH is the reciprocal of ACOSH.

COUNT(value1,value2,...)

Count. Counts the number of cells containing *values*. A maximum of 30 arguments containing values can exist.

COUNTA(value1,value2,...)

Count all. Counts the number of nonblank cells. A maximum of 30 arguments containing cell entries can exist.

DATE(year,month,day)

Date number. Returns a date from January 1, 1900, to December 31, 2078, as a serial number, where:

Date portion	Use
Year	00 – 178
Month	1 – 12
Day	1 – 31

DATEVALUE(date_text)

Date value. Returns *date_text* as a serial number.

DAVERAGE(database,field,criteria)

Database average. Calculates the average, or arithmetic mean, of the values in *field* of the *database* that matches the *criteria*.

DAY(serial_number)

Day of the month. Returns *serial_number* as a serial number from 1 to 31, the day of the month.

DAYS360(start_date,end_date)

Difference between 360 dates. Calculates the number of days between *start_date* and *end_date* as serial numbers, based on a 360-day financial calendar.

DB(cost,salvage,life,period,month)

Declining balance. Calculates the declining balance (real) depreciation of an asset for a specific period using the fixed-declining balance method. *Cost* is the original cost of the asset; *salvage* is the worth of the asset after depreciation; *life* is the number of periods in the length of the depreciation; *period* is one of the units of the length of the depreciation; *month* is the number of months for the first year. If omitted, *month* is 12.

DCOUNT(*database*,*field*,*criteria*)

Database count. Counts the number of cells containing values in *field* of the *database* that matches the *criteria*.

DCOUNTA(*database*,*field*,*criteria*)

Database count all. Counts the number of nonblank cells in *field* of the *database* that matches the *criteria*.

DDB(*cost*,*salvage*,*life*,*period*,*factor*)

Double-declining balance. Calculates the depreciation of an asset for a specific period using the double-declining balance method. *Cost* is the original cost of the asset; *salvage* is the worth of the asset after depreciation; *life* is the number of periods in the length of the depreciation; *period* is one of the units of the length of the depreciation; *factor* is the depreciation rate. If omitted, *factor* is 200%, an accelerated depreciation method.

DGET(*database*,*field*,*criteria*)

Database get. Extracts a single value based on *field* of the *database* that matches the *criteria*. No matching records result in #VALUE!, whereas multiple matching records result in #NUM!.

DMAX(*database*,*field*,*criteria*)

Database maximum. Returns the maximum value from *field* of the *database* that matches the *criteria*.

DMIN(*database*,*field*,*criteria*)

Database minimum. Returns the minimum value from *field* of the *database* that matches the *criteria*.

DOLLAR(*number*,*decimals*)

Number to text in currency format. Returns *number* as text rounded to the number of places specified in *decimals* and formatted with $#,##0.00_);($#,##0.00). *Decimals* rounds as follows:

Value	Result
Positive	Rounds to the right of the decimal point
Negative	Rounds to the left of the decimal point
Omitted	Rounds two places to the right of the decimal point

DPRODUCT(*database,field,criteria*)

Database product. Calculates the product of the values in the *field* of the *database* that matches the *criteria*.

DSTDEV(*database,field,criteria*)

Database sample standard deviation. Calculates an estimate for the standard deviation of a population based on a sample population, from *field* of the *database* that matches the *criteria*.

DSTDEVP(*database,field,criteria*)

Database population standard deviation. Calculates an estimate for the standard deviation of a population based on the entire population, from *field* of the *database* that matches the *criteria*.

DSUM(*database,field,criteria*)

Database sum. Calculates the total of values in the *field* of the *database* that matches the *criteria*.

DVAR(*database,field,criteria*)

Database sample variance. Calculates an estimate for the variance of a population based on a sample population, from *field* of the *database* that matches the *criteria*.

DVARP(*database,field,criteria*)

Database population variance. Calculates an estimate for the variance of a population based on the entire population, from *field* of the *database* that matches the *criteria*.

EXACT(*text1,text2*)

Exact comparison. Returns TRUE if *text1* and *text2* are exactly alike, returns FALSE if *text1* and *text2* are not exactly alike. Case of *text1* and *text2* must also match for TRUE.

EXP(*number*)

Exponent. Returns *e* to the power of *number,* where *e* equals 2.7182818. EXP is the reciprocal of the LN function.

FACT(*number*)

Factorial. Returns the factorial of *number*. A *number* with decimal places is truncated and then calculated.

FALSE()

False. Returns the logical value FALSE.

FIND(find_text,within_text,start_num)

Find text. Returns *find_text* from *within_text* beginning with the character specified by *start_num*. If *start_num* is omitted, 1 is used.

FIXED(number,decimals,no_comma)

Number to text with fixed decimal places. Returns *number* as text rounded to the number of places specified in *decimals,* with a comma separating thousands. *Decimals* rounds as follows:

Value	Result
Positive	Rounds to the right of the decimal point
Negative	Rounds to the left of the decimal point
Omitted	Rounds two places to the right of the decimal point

If *no_comma* is TRUE, commas are omitted; if *no_comma* is FALSE or omitted, commas are included.

FV(rate,nper,pmt,pv,type)

Future value. *Rate* is the interest rate; *nper* is the number of total payments; *pmt* is the amount of each payment; *pv* is the current total value; *type* is 1 or 0 to specify when payments are due. Calculates the future value of an annuity.

GROWTH(known_y's,known_x's,new_x's,const)

Exponential growth curve. Calculates an exponential growth curve based on the data *known_y's* and *known_x's and* then calculates y-values along the curve of the *new_x's* you specify. If *const* is omitted or TRUE, GROWTH calculates the constant term. If *const* is FALSE, *const* equals 1.

HLOOKUP(lookup_value,table_array, row_index_num)

Horizontal table lookup. Returns a value from *table_array* by searching the top row of *table_array* for *lookup_value* and then by searching down the corresponding column to the row specified in *row_index_number*. Cell contents of top row must be in ascending order. HLOOKUP uses the largest value that is less than *lookup_value* if *lookup_value* isn't present in *table_array*.

HOUR(serial_number)

Hour of the day. Returns *serial_number* (date-time code) as a serial number from 00 to 23, the hour of the 24-hour clock.

IF(logical_test,*value_if_true*,*value_if_false*)

If. Returns *value_if_true* if *logical_test* is TRUE; returns *value_if_false* if *logical_test* is FALSE. A maximum of seven nested IF functions can exist.

INDEX(array,*row_num*,*column_num*)

Horizontal and vertical table lookup. Returns a value from *array* based on value of *row_num* and *column_num*.

INDEX(reference,*row_num*,*column_num*, *area_num*)

Horizontal and vertical table lookup. Returns a cell reference from *area_num* based on the value of *row_num* and *column_num*. If *area_num* is omitted, INDEX uses area 1.

INDIRECT(ref_text,*a1*)

Indirect cell reference. Returns the contents of the cell referred from *ref_text*. If *a1* is TRUE or omitted, A1 reference style is used. If *a1* is FALSE, R1C1 reference style is used.

INFO(type_num)

Information about your Excel session. Returns information about your Excel session as specified by *type_num*. *Type_num* can be one of the following:

Type_num	Returns
"directory"	Current file directory
"memavail"	Amount of available random-access memory
"numfile"	Number of active spreadsheet files
"osversion"	Operating system version
"recalc"	Calculation mode (Automatic or Manual)
"release"	Microsoft Excel version number
"system"	Operating system name
"totmem"	Total random-access memory available, including memory in use, in bytes
"memused"	Amount of random-access memory use by data

INT(*number*)

Integer. Returns integer portion of *number,* by rounding down to the nearest integer. Effects the value and display of *number.*

IPMT(*rate,per,nper,pmt,pv,fv,type*)

Interest payment. Calculates the interest portion of a payment for an annuity. *Rate* is the interest rate; *per* is the interest period; *nper* is the number of total payment periods; *pmt* is amount of the payment; *pv* is the current total value; *fv* is the future value after the last payment; *type* is 1 or 0 specifying when the payment is due.

IRR(*values,guess*)

Internal rate of return. Calculates internal rate of return for a series of future cash flows (*values*). If omitted, *guess* (the estimated number) will be from .001 to .1.

ISBLANK(*value*)

Is blank? Returns TRUE if *value* is blank; returns FALSE if *value* is nonblank.

ISERR(*value*)

Is an error other than #N/A? Returns TRUE if *value* is an error other than #N/A; returns FALSE if *value* is anything else.

ISERROR(*value*)

Is an error value? Returns TRUE if *value* is an error value; returns FALSE if *value* is not an error value.

ISLOGICAL(*value*)

Is a logical value? Returns TRUE if *value* is a logical value; returns FALSE if *value* is not a logical value.

ISNA(*value*)

Is a #N/A? Returns TRUE if *value* is a #N/A error value; returns FALSE if *value* is not a #N/A error value.

ISNONTEXT(*value*)

Is not text? Returns TRUE if *value* is not text; returns FALSE if *value* is text.

ISNUMBER(value)

Is a number? Returns TRUE if *value* is a number; returns FALSE if *value* is not a number value.

ISREF(value)

Is a reference? Returns TRUE if *value* is a reference; returns FALSE if *value* is not a reference.

ISTEXT(value)

Is text? Returns TRUE if *value* is text; returns FALSE if *value* is not text.

LEFT(text,num_chars)

Left extract. Returns characters based on *num_chars* beginning at the far left of *text*. If *num_chars* is omitted, 1 is used.

LEN(text)

Length of text. Returns the number of characters in *text*.

LINEST(known_y's,known_x's,const,stats)

Linear estimate. Calculates the straight line that best fits your data using the least squares method and returns an array of data describing the line.

LN(number)

Natural logarithm. Returns the natural logarithm of *number* (base *e*), where *e* equals 2.7182818. LN is the reciprocal of EXP. LN of negative numbers or 0 returns the #NUM! error.

LOG(number,base)

Specified logarithm. Returns the logarithm of *number* in a *base* you specify. LOG of negative numbers or 0 returns the #NUM! error.

LOG10(number)

Standard logarithm. Returns the logarithm of *number* in base 10. LOG10 of negative numbers or 0 return the #NUM! error.

LOGEST(known_y's,known_x's,const,stats)

Logarithmic estimate. Calculates the exponential curve that fits your data and returns an array of data that describes the curve.

LOOKUP(lookup_value,lookup_vector, result_vector)

Horizontal or vertical vector lookup. Returns a value from *result_vector* based on searching *lookup_vector* using *lookup_value*. Both vectors are single rows or columns. *Lookup_vector* values must be in ascending order. LOOKUP uses the largest value that is less than *lookup_value* if *lookup_value* isn't present in *lookup_vector*.

LOOKUP(lookup_value,array)

Horizontal or vertical lookup. Returns a value or text from *array* based on *lookup_value*. LOOKUP searches for *lookup_value* across the top row if *array* has an equal number of rows and columns or more columns than rows and then returns the last value in the column. LOOKUP searches down the far left column if *array* has more rows than columns and then returns the last value in the row.

Cell contents must be in ascending order. LOOKUP uses the largest value that is less than *lookup_value* if *lookup_value* isn't present in *array*. LOOKUP (array format) is primarily for compatibility with other spreadsheet programs.

LOWER(text)

Lowercase conversion. Converts *text* to lowercase.

MATCH(lookup_value,lookup_array, match_type)

Matched value position. Returns the relative position of the value returned from *lookup_array* based on *lookup_value* and *match_type*. *Match_type* is the following:

Number	Result
1	Returns largest value that is less than or equal to *lookup_value*
0	Returns first value that is equal to *lookup_value*
–1	Returns smallest value that is greater than or equal to *lookup_value*

Match_type 1 and –1 require *lookup_array* to be in ascending order. If *match_type* is omitted, 1 is used.

*MAX(**number1**,number2,...)*

Maximum. Returns the maximum value from *numbers*. A maximum of 30 arguments can exist.

*MDETERM(**array**)*

Matrix determinant. Returns the matrix determinant of *array*.

*MEDIAN(**number1**,number2,...)*

Median. Returns the median, or middle, value from *numbers*. A maximum of 30 arguments can exist.

*MID(**text**,**start_num**,**num_chars**)*

Mid extract. Returns characters based on *num_chars* beginning with the character at *start_num* from *text*.

*MIN(**number1**,number2,...)*

Minimum. Returns the minimum value from *numbers*. A maximum of 30 arguments can exist.

*MINUTE(**serial_number**)*

Minute of the hour. Returns *serial_number* as a serial number from 00 to 59, the minute of the hour of the 24-hour clock.

*MINVERSE(**array**)*

Inverse matrix. Returns the inverse matrix of *array*.

*MIRR(**values**,**finance_rate**,**reinvest_rate**)*

Modified internal rate of return. Calculates modified internal rate of return. *Finance_rate* is the rate of the investment. *Reinvest_rate* is the rate positive cash flows can be reinvested.

*MMULT(**array1**,**array2**)*

Multiply matrix. Returns a new array based on the product of *array1* times *array2*.

MOD(number,divisor)

Modulo remainder. Returns the remainder (modulus) of the
result of the division of *number* by *divisor*. MOD returns the
#DIV/0 error when *divisor* equals 0. Use when you need to know
the quantity remaining from a division operation or to round out
to a specific day in a date formula.

MONTH(serial_number)

Month of the year. Returns *serial_number* as a serial number from
1 to 12, the months of the year.

N(value)

Number. Returns *value* as a number, where *value* is a number as
text or TRUE (1). Any other value is returned as 0.

NA()

Not available. Returns the error value #N/A!. Use as a place
marker in empty cells.

NOT(logical)

Not. Returns TRUE if *logical* is false; returns FALSE if *logical* is
true.

NOW()

Current date and time. Returns the date and time serial number
based on your computer's clock. Date and time are updated when
you open the spreadsheet or calculate the spreadsheet containing NOW.

NPER(rate,pmt,pv,fv,type)

Number of periods. Calculates the number of periods needed to
achieve the specified annuity.

NPV(rate,value1,value2,...)

Net present value. Calculates the net present value of future cash
flows (*value1,value2,...*) discounted at *rate*. If your first cash flow
occurs at the beginning of the first period, use this formula:

```
=NPV(rate,value2,value3,...)+value1
```

OFFSET(**reference,row,cols,***height,width*)

Cell reference offset. Returns a reference offset from *reference* specified by the number of *rows* and *cols,* optionally with a specified *height* and *width*. If *height* and *width* are omitted, reference height and width are used.

OR(**logical1,***logical2,...*)

Or. Returns TRUE if one or more arguments are true; returns FALSE if all arguments are false.

PI()

π. Returns the value of pi, 3.14159265358979. Use when you need to calculate the number of radians in an angle, using the formula `Radians =PI()*Degrees/180`.

PMT(**rate,nper,pv,***fv,type*)

Payment. Calculates the periodic payment amount for an annuity.

PPMT(**rate,per,nper,pv,***fv,type*)

Principal payment. Calculates the principal portion of a payment for an annuity.

PRODUCT(**number1,***number2,...*)

Product of numbers. Returns product of *number1* by *number2,* and so on for remaining arguments. PRODUCT can multiply a maximum of 30 arguments that are values.

PROPER(**text**)

Proper case conversion. Converts the first letter of *text* to uppercase and all other characters to lowercase.

RAND()

Random number. Returns a random decimal number from 0 to 1. A new random number is returned if you press the F9 key or choose either Options⇨Calculation⇨Calc Now or Calc Document.

RATE(**rate,nper,pmt,pv,***type*)

Rate. Calculates the interest rate for an annuity.

REPLACE(old_text,start_num,num_chars, new_text)

Replace portion of text. Exchanges the characters in *old_text* with *new_text* beginning with the character specified by *start_num* and continuing for the number of characters specified by *num_characters*.

REPT(text,num_times)

Repeat text. Duplicates *text* the amount specified in *num_times*.

RIGHT(text,num_chars)

Right extract. Returns characters based on *num_chars* beginning at the far right of *text*. If *num_chars* is omitted, 1 is used.

ROUND(number,num_digits)

Round off. Returns *number* rounded to the number of places specified in *num_digits*. A positive *num_digits* rounds up the number of places to the right of the decimal point; a negative *num_digits* rounds up the number of places to the left of the decimal point; and a 0 *num_digits* rounds to the integer of *number*. This function affects the display and value of *number*.

ROW (reference)

Row number. Returns the row number of the cell *reference*. A multiple cell reference returns a vertical array of row numbers. If *reference* is omitted, the row number of ROW's cell address is returned.

ROWS(array)

Number of rows. Returns the number of rows in *array*.

SEARCH(find_text,within_text,start_num)

Search for text. Returns the character number where *find_text* begins from *within_text,* beginning at *start_num*. If *start_num* is omitted, 1 is used.

SECOND(serial_number)

Second of the minute. Returns *serial_number* as a serial number from 00 to 59, the second of the minute of the 24-hour clock.

SIGN(number)

Determine sign. Returns 1 if *number* is positive, –1 if *number* is negative, and 0 if *number* is 0.

SIN(number)

Sine. Returns the sine of radian angle *number*. SIN is the reciprocal of ASIN.

SINH(number)

Hyperbolic sine. Returns the hyperbolic sine of *number*. SINH is the reciprocal of ASINH.

SLN(cost,salvage,life)

Straight-line. Calculates the depreciation of an asset per period using the straight-line method.

SQRT(number)

Square root. Returns the square root of a positive *number*. A negative *number* returns the #NUM! error.

STDEV(number1,number2,...)

Sample standard deviation. Calculates an estimate for the standard deviation of a population from a sample from the population. A maximum of 30 arguments can exist.

STDEVP(number1,number2,...)

Population standard deviation. Calculates an estimate for the standard deviation of a population from the entire population. A maximum of 30 arguments can exist.

SUBSTITUTE(text,old_text,new_text, instance_num)

Substitute portion of text. Exchanges characters in *old_text* for characters *new_text* in *text* the number of times specified in *instance_num*. If *instance_num* is omitted, each instance of *old_text* is exchanged for *new_text*.

SUM(number1,number2,...)

Sum. Calculates the total of *numbers*.

SUMPRODUCT(array1,array2,...)

Sumproduct. Multiplies the corresponding cell in each array and totals the products. Each array must have the same number of rows and columns, or SUMPRODUCT returns #VALUE!.

SYD(cost,salvage,life,period)

Sum-of-the-year's digits. Calculates the depreciation of an asset for a specific period using the sum-of-the-year's digits method, which is an accelerated depreciation method.

T(value)

Text equivalent. Returns the equivalent text of *value*.

TAN(number)

Tangent. Returns the tangent of radian angle *number*. TAN is the reciprocal of ATAN.

TANH(number)

Hyperbolic tangent. Returns the hyperbolic tangent of *number*. TANH is the reciprocal of ATANH.

TEXT(value,format_text)

Value to text conversion. Returns *value* as text and displays text using *format_text*. *Format_text* uses the same codes as Format Number.

TIME(hour,minute,second)

Time number. Returns a time as a serial number, using a 24-hour clock (military time), where:

Time portion	Use
Hour	0 – 23
Minute	0 – 59
Second	0 – 59

TIMEVALUE(time_text)

Time value. Returns *time_text* as a serial number.

TODAY()

Today's number. Returns the date based on your computer's clock. The date is updated when you open the spreadsheet or calculate the spreadsheet containing TODAY.

TRANSPOSE(*array*)

Transpose array. Returns a new array that has *array*'s first row as its first column, *array*'s second row as its second column, and so on.

TREND(***known_y's***,*known_x's*,*new_x's*,*const*)

Trend. Calculates the straight line that best fits your data using the least squares method and returns an array of data describing the line.

TRIM(***text***)

Trim text. Returns *text* with blank spaces removed from the beginning, end, and between words so that only one space separates words.

TRUE()

True. Returns the logical value TRUE.

TRUNC(***number***,*num_digits*)

Truncate integers. Returns integer portion of *number*, by removing all digits to the right of the decimal point. This function affects the value and display of *number*.

TYPE(*value*)

Cell content type. Returns the type of cell contents, as follows:

Cell content	Result
Number	1
Text	2
Logical value	4
Error value	16
Array	64

UPPER(*text*)

Uppercase conversion. Converts *text* to uppercase.

VALUE(*text*)

Text to value conversion. Returns *text* formatted as a number or date to values. Use for compatibility with other spreadsheet programs.

VAR(***number1***,*number2*,...)

Sample variance. Calculates an estimate for the variance of a population based on a sample of the population. A maximum of 30 arguments can exist.

VARP(***number1***,*number2*,...)

Population variance. Calculates an estimate for the variance of a population based on the entire population. A maximum of 30 arguments can exist.

VDB(***cost,salvage,life,start_period, end_period***,*factor,no_switch*)

Variable-declining balance. Calculates the depreciation of an asset for a specific period using the 200% (or other factor) double-declining balance method. *Factor* is the depreciation rate. If omitted, *factor* is 200%. *Start_period* and *end_period* are the beginning and ending times for the specific period. *No_switch* determines whether VDB switches to straight-line depreciation. If *no_switch* is TRUE, VDB does not switch to straight-line. If *no_switch* is FALSE or omitted, VDB switches to straight-line. An accelerated depreciation method.

VLOOKUP(***lookup_value,table_array, col_index_num***)

Vertical table lookup. Returns a value from *table_array* by searching the far left column of *table_array* for *lookup_value* and then by searching across the corresponding row to the column specified in *col_index_number*. Cell contents of the far left column must be in ascending order. VLOOKUP uses the largest value that is less than *lookup_value* if *lookup_value* isn't present in *table_array*.

WEEKDAY(serial_number)

Day of the week. Returns *serial_number* as the day of the week, where 1 = Sunday and 7 = Saturday.

YEAR(serial_number)

Year. Returns *serial_number* as the year, from 0 to 199 (1900 – 2099).

Part VI:
The Dummies Guide to
Excel's Keyboard Commands

Mice are nice, but keys are a breeze. If you're entering data at the keyboard, you'll lose valuable seconds by removing your hand from the keyboard, groping for the mouse, and then dragging it around looking for the right place to click.

After you get the hang of a few essential keyboard commands, you'll probably find yourself using the mouse less and less. Maybe not. In any case, I've compiled listings of the most useful keyboard shortcuts.

Moving Through the Worksheet

Key(s)	Operation
Arrow keys ($\rightarrow \leftarrow \uparrow \downarrow$)	Moves left, right, up, down one cell.
Home	Moves to the beginning of the row.
PgUp	Moves up one screenful.
Ctrl+PgUp	Moves left one screenful.
PgDn	Moves down one screenful.
Ctrl+PgDn	Moves right one screenful.
Ctrl+Home	Moves to the first cell in the worksheet (A1).
Ctrl+End	Moves to the last active cell of the worksheet.
Ctrl+Arrow key	Moves to the edge of a data block. If the cell is blank, moves to the first nonblank cell.
F5	Prompts for a cell address to go to.

Selecting Cells in the Worksheet

Key(s)	Operation
Shift+Arrow key	Expands the selection in the direction indicated.
Shift+Spacebar	Selects the entire row.
Ctrl+Spacebar	Selects the entire column.
Ctrl+Shift+Spacebar	Selects the entire worksheet.
Shift+Home	Expands the selection to the beginning of the current row.
Ctrl+* (asterisk)	Selects the block of data surrounding the active cell.
F8	Extends the selection as you use navigation keys.
Shift+F8	Adds other nonadjacent cells or ranges to the selection. Pressing Shift+F8 again ends the Add mode.
F5	Prompts for a range or range name to select.

Moving Around Within a Range Selection

Key(s)	Operation
Enter	Moves the cell pointer to the next cell down in the selection.
Shift+Enter	Moves the cell pointer to the previous cell up in the selection.
Tab	Moves the cell pointer to the next cell to the right in the selection.
Shift+Tab	Moves the cell pointer to the previous cell to the left in the selection.
Ctrl+. (period)	Moves to the next corner of the current cell range.
Ctrl+Tab	Moves to the next cell range in a nonadjacent selection.
Ctrl+Shift+Tab	Moves to the previous cell range in a nonadjacent selection.
Shift+Backspace	Collapses the cell selection to just the active cell.

Using the Editing Keys in the Formula Bar

Key(s)	Operation
F2	Begins editing the active cell.
Arrow keys ($\uparrow \downarrow \rightarrow \leftarrow$)	Moves the cursor one character in the direction of the arrow.
Home	Moves the cursor to the beginning of the line.
End	Moves the cursor to the end of the line.
Ctrl+$\rightarrow$	Moves the cursor one word to the right.
Ctrl+$\leftarrow$	Moves the cursor one word to the left.
Delete	Deletes the character to the right of the cursor.
Ctrl+Delete	Deletes all characters from the cursor to the end of the line.
Backspace	Deletes the character to the left of the cursor.

Using the Formatting Keys

Key(s)	Operation
Ctrl+1	Applies normal format.
Ctrl+B	Sets or removes boldface.
Ctrl+I	Sets or removes italic.
Ctrl+U	Sets or removes underlining.
Ctrl+S	Activates the style box on the Standard toolbar.
Ctrl+Shift+~	Applies the general number format.
Ctrl+Shift+!	Applies the comma format with two decimal places.
Ctrl+Shift+#	Applies the date format.
Ctrl+Shift+$	Applies the currency format with two decimal places.
Ctrl+Shift+%	Applies the percent format with no decimal places.

Applying Other Shortcut Keys

Key(s)	Operation
Ctrl+X	Edit⇨Cut command.
Ctrl+Delete	Edit⇨Cut command.
Ctrl+C	Edit⇨Copy command.
Ctrl+Insert	Edit⇨Copy command.
Ctrl+V	Edit⇨Paste command.
Shift+Insert	Edit⇨Paste command.
Ctrl+Z	Edit⇨Undo command.
Alt+Backspace	Edit⇨Undo command.
Ctrl+R	Edit⇨Fill Right command.
Ctrl+D	Edit⇨Fill Left [h] command.
Delete	Edit⇨Clear command.

Using the Function Keys

Key(s)	What it does
F1	Help⇨Contents command.
Shift+F1	Summons context-sensitive help.
Alt+F1	File⇨New command (Chart).
Alt+Shift+F1	File⇨New command (Worksheet).
Alt+Ctrl+F1	File⇨New command (Macro Sheet).
F2	Enables you to edit the active cell.
Shift+F2	Formula⇨Note command.
Ctrl+F2	Options⇨Workspace⇨Info Window command.
Alt+F2	File⇨Save As command.
Alt+Shift+F2	File⇨Save command.
Alt+Ctrl+F2	File⇨Open command.
Alt+Ctrl+Shift+F2	File⇨Print command.
F3	Formula⇨Paste Name command.
Shift+F3	Formula⇨Paste Function command.
Ctrl+F3	Formula⇨Define Name command.
Ctrl+Shift+F3	Formula⇨Create Names command.
F4	Changes cell reference while you edit a formula.
Ctrl+F4	File⇨Close command.
Alt+F4	File⇨Exit command.
F5	Formula⇨Goto command.
Shift+F5	Formula⇨Find command.
Ctrl+F5	Restores a minimized document window to its previous size.
F6	Moves to the next pane in a split window.
Shift+F6	Moves to the previous pane in a split window.
Ctrl+F6	Activates the next open window.
Ctrl+Shift+F6	Activates the previous open window.
F7	Repeats the previous Formula⇨Find command.

Key(s)	What it does
Shift+F7	Repeats the previous Formula⇨Find command but finds the previous occurrence.
Ctrl+F7	Enables you to move the current window with the arrow keys.
F8	Toggles selection Extend mode on and off.
Shift+F8	Toggles selection Add mode on and off.
Ctrl+F8	Enables you to resize the current window with the arrow keys.
F9	Recalculates all open worksheets.
Shift+F9	Recalculates the current worksheet.
Ctrl+F9	Minimizes the current window.
F10	Activates the menu bar.
Shift+F10	Activates the shortcut menu (simulates right-clicking).
Ctrl+F10	Maximizes the current window.
F11	File⇨New command (Chart).
Shift+F11	File⇨New command (Worksheet).
Ctrl+F11	File⇨New command (Macro Sheet).
F12	File⇨Save As command.
Shift+F12	File⇨Save command.
Ctrl+F12	File⇨Open command.
Ctrl+Shift+F12	File⇨Print command.

Index

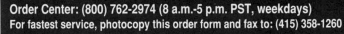

Order Form

Order Center: (800) 762-2974 (8 a.m.-5 p.m. PST, weekdays)
For fastest service, photocopy this order form and fax to: (415) 358-1260

Qty	ISBN	Title	Price	Total

Shipping & Handling Charges

Subtotal	U.S.	Canada & International	International Air Mail
Up to $20.00	Add $3.00	Add $4.00	Add $10.00
$20.01-40.00	$4.00	$5.00	$20.00
$40.01-60.00	$5.00	$6.00	$25.00
$60.01-80.00	$6.00	$8.00	$35.00
Over $80.00	$7.00	$10.00	$50.00

In U.S. and Canada, shipping is UPS ground or equivalent.
For Rush shipping call (800) 762-2974.

Subtotal _____

CA residents add
applicable sales tax _____

IN residents add
5% sales tax _____

Canadian residents
add 7% GST tax _____

Shipping _____

TOTAL _____

Ship to:

Name _____

Company _____

Address _____

City/State/Zip _____

Daytime Phone _____

Payment: ❏ Check to IDG Books (US Funds Only) ❏ Visa ❏ MasterCard ❏ AMEX

Card # _____ Exp. _____

Signature _____

Please send this order form to: IDG Books, 155 Bovet Road, Suite 310, San Mateo, CA 94402.
Allow up to 3 weeks for delivery. Thank you!

IDG BOOKS WORLDWIDE REGISTRATION CARD

RETURN THIS REGISTRATION CARD FOR FREE CATALOG

Title of this book: Excel For Dummies Quick Reference

My overall rating of this book: ❏ Very good [1] ❏ Good [2] ❏ Satisfactory [3] ❏ Fair [4] ❏ Poor [5]

How I first heard about this book:

❏ Found in bookstore; name: [6]

❏ Book review: [7]

❏ Advertisement: [8]

❏ Catalog: [9]

❏ Word of mouth; heard about book from friend, co-worker, etc.: [10] ❏ Other: [11]

What I liked most about this book:

What I would change, add, delete, etc., in future editions of this book:

Other comments:

Number of computer books I purchase in a year: ❏ 1 [12] ❏ 2-5 [13] ❏ 6-10 [14] ❏ More than 10 [15]

I would characterize my computer skills as: ❏ Beginner [16] ❏ Intermediate [17] ❏ Advanced [18] ❏ Professional [19]

I use ❏ DOS [20] ❏ Windows [21] ❏ OS/2 [22] ❏ Unix [23] ❏ Macintosh [24] ❏ Other: [25]_____
(please specify)

I would be interested in new books on the following subjects:

(please check all that apply, and use the spaces provided to identify specific software)

❏ Word processing: [26]

❏ Spreadsheets: [27]

❏ Data bases: [28]

❏ Desktop publishing: [29]

❏ File Utilities: [30]

❏ Money management: [31]

❏ Networking: [32]

❏ Programming languages: [33]

❏ Other: [34]

I use a PC at (please check all that apply): ❏ home [35] ❏ work [36] ❏ school [37] ❏ other: [38] _____

The disks I prefer to use are ❏ 5.25 [39] ❏ 3.5 [40] ❏ other: [41]_____

I have a CD ROM: ❏ yes [42] ❏ no [43]

I plan to buy or upgrade computer hardware this year: ❏ yes [44] ❏ no [45]

I plan to buy or upgrade computer software this year: ❏ yes [46] ❏ no [47]

Name: _____ Business title: [48]

Type of Business: [49]

Address (❏ home [50] ❏ work [51]/Company name: _____)

Street/Suite#

City [52]/State [53]/Zipcode [54]: _____ Country [55]

IDG BOOKS

THE WORLD OF COMPUTER KNOWLEDGE

❏ **I liked this book!**
You may quote me by name in future IDG Books Worldwide promotional materials.

My daytime phone number is _____

❏ **YES!**
Please keep me informed about IDG's World
of Computer Knowledge. Send me the latest
IDG Books catalog.